HUMAN NEEDS AND REGIONAL DEVELOPMENT

UNITED NATIONS CENTRE FOR REGIONAL DEVELOPMENT
REGIONAL DEVELOPMENT SERIES

Edited by M. Honjo and R. P. Misra

Volume 7: Human Needs and Regional Development

Edited by Haruo Nagamine

The contents of this volume are drawn from papers contributed by UNCRD staff and consultants in various seminars, meetings, etc., and from the country reports of UNCRD's pilot study on Planning for Basic Needs at the Microlevel.

Opinion expressed in various sections of this volume are those of the authors and do not necessarily reflect those of the United Nations Secretariat or of the United Nations Centre for Regional Development.

Designations employed and presentation of material in this publication do not imply the expression of any opinion whatsoever on the part of the United Nations Secretariat or the United Nations Centre for Regional Development concerning legal status of any country or territory, city or area, or of its authorities, or concerning the delimitation of its frontiers or boundaries.

HUMAN NEEDS AND REGIONAL DEVELOPMENT

Edited by
Haruo Nagamine

MARUZEN ASIA
For and on behalf of the United Nations Centre for Regional Development
Nagoya, Japan

ISBN 962-220-207-1
Distributed by
Maruzen Asia Pte. Ltd.,
P O Box 67 Pasir Panjang,
Singapore 9111.

Printed in the Republic of Singapore
by Huntsmen Offset Printing Pte. Ltd.

FOREWORD

THIS IS the seventh volume of the UNCRD Regional Development Series. The earlier volumes dealt with changing perception of development problems, regional development alternatives, national development and regional policy, rural development and regional policy, rural-urban relations and regional development and urbanization. This volume is concerned with basic human needs as an essential dimension of local and regional development.

Concern about basic human needs emerged from the growing realization that economic growth does not necessarily ensure development — when the latter is seen in its broader and more realistic perspectives. The structural rigidities of the human society and human social behaviour do not allow the benefits of growth to trickle down to those who need them most — the poor and underprivileged. Development must therefore have a two-pronged objective — economic growth and social equity.

Unfortunately not enough effort was made to conceptualize and operationalize the concept of basic human needs before its incorporation in the national plans of the developing countries. Lack of clarity has led to several misconceptions and doubts which continue to prevail in many circles and it is partly reflected in some of the papers included in the volume. One thing that is clear now, if it needed clarity, is that BMN is not a substitute for economic growth, nor is it planning for consumption needs. It however calls for a new style of development wherein economic growth becomes the means rather than the end of development.

As mentioned earlier, there has been considerable divergence in views about the ways by which the basic human needs be conceptualized, identified and operationalized. The purpose of this volume is not to advocate any single approach for this important but somewhat controversial concept, but to present the wide range of dimensions in which the concept can be made use of for the solution of real-world problems.

The volume contains several theoretical papers contributed by well-known authorities. Further, it introduces some efforts for operationalizing the concept of basic human needs at the microarea levels in India, the Republic of Korea, Nepal, Pakistan and the Philippines.

We are grateful to Haruo Nagamine, Physical Planner at UNCRD for editing this volume and thus contributing immensely to the success of the UNCRD Series on Regional Development. We would also like to take this opportunity to thank all those who have contributed papers included in this volume.

We are confident that the volume will be a welcome addition to the growing literature on the concept of basic human needs and its application to planning for socioeconomic development.

M. Honjo and R. P. Misra

PREFACE

AT THE Colloquium on the Methods of Planning for Comprehensive Regional Development held in October 1976 at the United Nations Centre for Regional Development (UNCRD), concerns were expressed by many participants about the need to operationalize the concept of basic human needs for planning at the grassroots level. In response to this, UNCRD sponsored pilot studies on Planning for Basic Needs at the Microarea Level, in collaboration with Institute of Development Studies, University of Mysore, India; Graduate School of Environmental Studies, Seoul National University, Seoul; Chonnam National University, Kwangju, Republic of Korea and Region XI Office, National Economic Development Authority (NEDA), the Government of the Philippines. Part of the findings of these studies, most relevant to the theme of this volume, is introduced in some of the chapters of this volume. The volume contains several papers prepared by well-known authorities for various seminars and meetings of the UNCRD touching on the social aspects of regional development.

I would like to take this opportunity to express my gratitude to the authors of these papers and reports. I am particularly thankful to two very close friends of mine who helped me immensely as consultants to the research project: Kazuo Koike, Professor, Labour Relations, Faculty of Economics, Nagoya University, Japan; and Shoaib Sultan Khan of Pakistan, working at present as a rural development expert, UNICEF, Sri Lanka.

I am also indebted to several other colleagues who helped me in many ways: Kenji Oya and Mitsuhiko Hosaka, research associates, as project team members of the study; Ed. B. Prantilla, Om P. Mathur and particularly, Josefa S. Edralin for the final editing; Fumiko Takeyama, Sumiko Torii and Frances Miwa for diligently typing several drafts of the papers, and above all, Hiroko Okada for her devotion and commitment in secretarial assistance and typewriting.

Nagoya, Japan   Haruo Nagamine
27 December 1980

CONTENTS

Foreword . . . . (v)
Preface . . . . (vii)
1 Introduction
   — *Haruo Nagamine* 1
2 Measurement of Basic Minimum Needs
   — *United Nations Secretariat* 11
3 Basic Needs and Development Planning:
Focus on India and the Philippines
   — *R.P. Misra and Ed. B. Prantilla* 33
4 The Saemaul Movement and the Concept of Basic Needs
   — *Sang-Chuel Choe* 69
5 Planning for Children and Women in Regional Development
   — *Mujib R. Khan* 89
6 Local Level Planning: The Pakistan Experience
   — *Shoaib Sultan Khan* 101
7 Innovation in the Health Delivery System:
An Integrated Approach to Planning
   — *Ed. B. Prantilla and Aurora R. Pelayo* 129
8 A Case Study of Basic Needs in Nepal
   — *Jiro Kawakita* 161
9 The Disenthronement of Basic Needs:
Twenty Questions
   — *Benjamin Higgins* 175
10 Studying the Basic Needs at the Microarea Level:
A Methodological Note
   — *Haruo Nagamine* 227
Bibliography 245
Contributors 267
Index 269

1

INTRODUCTION

HARUO NAGAMINE

MEETING THE basic human needs has been one of the implicitly accepted prime goals of planning in developing countries. In explicit terms, however, it acquired necessary and worldwide attention only during the Second Development Decade (1970–79). The failure of growth-oriented development planning to improve the well-being of the poor and consequent questioning of the goals of development policies pursued by developing countries and to some extent even developed countries, led to the emergence of basic human needs as a prime consideration in national development efforts.

The concept of basic human needs often refers to the satisfaction of some essential requirements for a human being to live under conditions compatible with human dignity. Thus, to start with, it has to deal with commonly accepted standards for the level of living, consisting of food, clothing, shelter, health, education, social security, working conditions and human liberty. The concept is time, place and culture specific.

According to the International Labour Organization (ILO), the basic needs approach means not only the provision of a minimum level of security to all individuals but the creation of conditions that will allow continuing equal access to opportunities for self-sufficiency and self-sustained growth in the course of the development process."[1] Styles of development processes implied by this strategy are those which can "generate rates of economic growth which will allow for continued expansion of employment, and to redirect production patterns towards basic goods and services."[2] Thus, the strategy does not disregard at all the importance of economic growth and employment; it attempts to see that the fruits of development reach underprivileged sections of the society. More concretely, the ILO approach to basic needs is directed to:

[1] Franklyn Lisk and Diane Werneke, *Alternative Development Strategies and Basic Needs* (Geneva: International Labour Office, 1976) (Economic and Social Policy Synthesis Programme Working Paper).
[2] Ibid.

1. provide an increase in the income and productivity of the poor to make available basic consumption goods and to provide the means to acquire them;
2. provide an increase in basic public services to the poorest segments of the population, primarily in rural areas, but also in urban fringe areas;
3. redress the biases which presently favour the modern urban sector against the rural and urban traditional sectors; and
4. generate adequate growth to meet needs and carry the strategy forward over time.[3]

This approach looks at the basic needs issue from the point of view of production of goods and services and their distribution favouring the poor and underprivileged. Comprehensive as it may appear in its outlook, the approach basically emphasizes economic considerations. It is not inappropriate to give greater weight to economic factors in the short run, in the light of the fact that no matter what the deficiencies in the institutional system, provision of those goods and services which enter the basic needs basket can never be ensured without a corresponding increase in production of those goods and services. But we cannot forget the apparent mutual causation among the factors involved in the basic needs paradigm. For instance, while the state of health is considered a social aspect, it is an essential prerequisite for a person to be economically active. Similarly, the fruits of production cannot bring about welfare of all unless there is an effective institutional mechanism for distributive justice. As such, it is rather difficult to identify one particular aspect as more important than others except in very specific contexts. We have also to keep in view the fact that developing countries still suffer from a number of institutional infirmities which are counter-developmental in nature. Their negative effect often being so far-reaching that their eradication justifiably seems to be one of the essentials of development.[4] Successful experiences in rural development in Asia in recent years, such as the Saemaul Undong of the Republic of Korea or the Sarvodaya Shramadana movement of Sri Lanka seem to endorse this observation; both of them clearly suggest the importance of institutional (social, cultural and political) factors (i.e., enlightened village leadership, effective response from the government to the aspiration of people at the microarea level, a moral approach to generate devotion and sense of commitment, and reawakening of

---

[3] Ibid.
[4] The United Nations Economic and Social Council (ECOSOC) resolution 1582 (L) of May 1971 defines the objectives of regional development. Out of five items mentioned, three refer to institutional changes.

nonmaterialistic values over materialistic values that dominate the world today) in triggering viable processes of self-reliant development.

Physical aspects (locational, spatial, environmental and infrastructural) appear to be another influential factor that affects the nature of development as well as the basic needs of a community, perhaps more so at a stage where infrastructures are still inadequate (in a more advanced situation, locational disadvantages are considerably offset by efficient transport and communication systems). Proximity of a village to a market centre may stimulate some development — positive or negative. People will have better access to additional income-earning opportunities through employment generated in the market centre, and/or through additional productive activities in the village as a response to consumptive demands from the market centre. Their felt needs for material well-being will be expanded through demonstration effects; interest in educating their dependents, so that their next generation become more viable partners in modern sectors, will be strengthened. At the same time, various forms of "social illnesses" will also infiltrate the village.

Furthermore, it is not difficult to appreciate the extent to which other physical conditions can affect the basic needs profile of a community; availability of land for cultivation as well as other types of natural resources and various climatic conditions are just a few of them. Thus, it is essential to consider these aspects as independent variables in the paradigm of basic human needs together with economic factors. This perception would be particularly relevant in the context of a longer-range time frame. The importance of a long-range oriented paradigm should be recognized for few less developed countries would be able to attain basic needs goals within a short-range time frame.

From a wider perspective, what we are pursuing after all is harmonious *development*. Consequently we should consider two essential criteria to determine the strategies for development, i.e., economic viability and sociopolitical acceptability.[5] Accordingly, development planning means the formulation schemes of allocation and mobilization of all developmental resources (financial, physical, human and institutional) for attaining a mixture of goals which, while accommodating the two basic criteria above, represent a specific choice of a society to be made through its political processes. Fulfilment of these two essential criteria must reconcile problems of trade-off in terms of resource allocation, particularly in a short-range time frame.[6] Hence, when we translate basic developmental ideologies and policies

---

[5] Haruo Nagamine, "Methods of Planning for Comprehensive Regional Development: A Paradigm," *Asian Development Dialogue*, No. 5 and 6 (1977) p. 6.
[6] Ibid.

chosen by the society into a concrete scheme of resource allocation (i.e., development planning), there is a need for an *operational guideline* through which all the sectors that constitute development are assured of critical minimum levels of fulfilment, so that an acceptable and feasible compromise for the trade-off between the two essential goals of development is obtained. It is proposed that the concept of basic human needs, in fact, is a criterion that serves as this kind of operational guideline for development planning.[7]

Meanwhile it should be recognized that all the factors that constitute the paradigm of basic needs are internal to that of development; the concept of basic needs therefore is an expression of an explicit choice in the style of development. Hence, some fallacies should be definitely avoided, such as considering basic needs as a new independent sector, or to see it as something external to the concept of development itself.

As such the concept of basic human needs should not be limited to a set of standards in terms of food, nutrition, clothing, shelter, education and health alone. Mere supply of goods and services is not enough. The concept should incorporate all essential requirements in terms of financial, physical, human (technological) and institutional resources for bringing about viable processes of self-reliant development at various levels of government (village, district, province, region and nation), vis-à-vis constraints in terms of availability of these resources. The basic needs should thus include financial capital, land, technologies appropriate to prevalent levels of the people's capability, labour supply conditions, entrepreneurship, physical resource potentials to be tapped for additional income-earning activities, as well as identification of local demands and market conditions, availability of key infrastructures that may allow for new introduction/expansion of viable productive activities and various institutional arrangements that will ensure proper mobilization of needed resources. Other factors may also be included.

One special element of basic needs which links economic and sociopolitical factors is employment. It serves as an essential distributive mechanism through which the fruits of development (those attained through viable economic goals) reach all the quarters of the society in question, particularly its weaker sections.

[7] Lisk and Werneke, "Alternative Development Strategies and Basic Needs," p. 48.

Multilevel Structure

All basic human needs cannot be provided for and planned for each individual or family. For example, food, clothing and shelter, the three primary basic needs, have to be planned for each individual and/or family. Many others like health and education can be only community based. Such services, however, cannot be made available to each small community. The nature, as well as quantity, of various basic needs components would vary from one spatio-government unit to another. There is however no single administrative (i.e., spatial) unit that can cope with all the basic needs requirements within itself. Wholesome functioning of a community can be materialized only when various hierarchical units of the country function in a cohesive and mutually complementary manner. This points to the importance of identifying the hierarchical structure of functions among all levels of communities in dealing with basic needs as a whole. In this volume, our focus will be on those basic needs components which have to be provided at the microarea level in the rural areas, i.e., a group of villages, a village, the subdivisions of a village, as well as individual households and individuals.

Subjective versus Objective Dimensions

All basic needs have dual facets, i.e., objective (normative) and subjective (perceptive).[8] Attendance of children in elementary schools may be one of the important components from a normative point of view, but there may be more important activities to be done by children from the point of view of some villagers. Food preference of a group of people may contradict the normative dietary requirements. The Government may consider provision of an access road to a village to be most important, but the villagers may put priority on something else. Anyway, there is no universally applicable formula to reconcile these discrepancies, except untiring efforts at dialogue between the community and government towards situation-specific, group-specific and area-specific solutions. Learning processes involved in such dialogues will have profound implications in bringing the development planning closer to the needs of the people.

---

[8] United Nations Secretariat, "Measurement of Basic Minimum Needs," *Asian Development Dialogue*, No. 5 and 6, (1977); reprinted in Chapter 2.

Temporal Dimension

On account of various socioeconomic forces operating in a society, quantity as well as quality of basic needs is bound to change over time.[9] This applies to both normative and subjective components. While subjective needs are quite susceptible to changes by demonstrable effects, normative requirements also change commensurate with the overall societal progress. Requirements for a minimum level of educational attainment for example, cannot remain the same. Changes in market will also impose changes in productive technologies and marketing practices employed by a community or an organization. A conceptual framework for basic human needs discussed above is presented in a diagrammatic form in Figure 1-1.

Operational Dimensions

While Figure 1-1 indicates the various factors that constitute the basic human needs in relation to the ultimate goal of development, it is useful to classify basic needs into four broad areas of concern as a means to examine the operational dimensions of basic needs. These areas are as follows:
1. those relative to personal consumption;
2. those relative to essential social services;
3. those relative to productive capability, and
4. others, such as human liberty and participation in decision-making.

These four areas are complementary rather than mutually exclusive. For example, simply catering to personal consumption without augmenting production capability will degenerate into mere perpetuation of spoon-feeding; by the same token, strengthening of production capability that would not contribute to betterment of personal consumption would mean continuous exploitation of the poor.

Nonetheless, this classification would be helpful for articulating policy priorities that would be necessary even among the bare minimum components of basic needs. In many situations, what a developing country could afford would be little more than concentrating its efforts for strengthening productive capability of, and providing essential social services for the target groups simply because of resource constraints. Otherwise the ultimate goal of development — self-reliance — would never be brought about.

---

[9] This concept relates to the notion of the hierarchy of needs, advocated by A. H. Maslow, see Ibid.

Figure 1-1. Paradigm of Basic Human Needs
Change of BHN over Time Induced by Development Progress

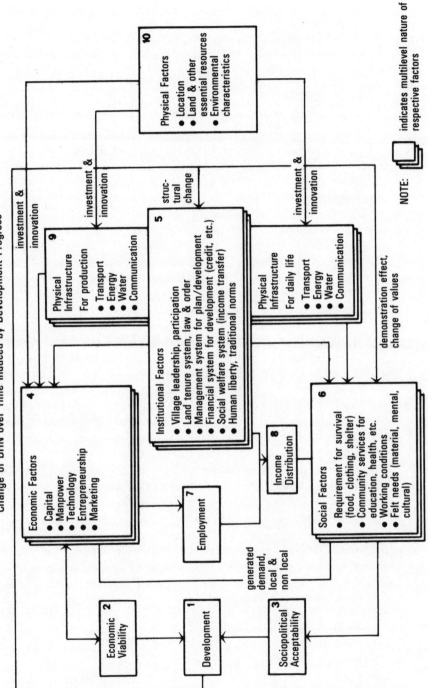

NOTE: ⬚ indicates multilevel nature of respective factors

The above point would also have crucial bearing on the way we should translate into planning terms, the needs and aspirations as perceived by the people themselves. For people who are extremely poor, it may often be difficult to conceive of their essential needs beyond the bare necessities of personal consumption, such as what to eat tomorrow or the minimum amount of drinking water for mere survival.

However, except for situations that may justify direct relief measures (e.g., food rations for an area experiencing famine), one can safely generalize that the correct solution should be sought in terms of strengthening productive capability and essential social services rather than direct attendance to personal consumption.

Another essential dimension to be kept in mind when translating the concept of basic human needs into development planning is the level of actions through which those needs are effectively and eventually met. Many problems which contribute to the failure to meet basic human needs of the poor are so fundamental that very few can be solved without government commitment. Implementation of land reform is a typical example. Without ensuring more equitable access to land, the most essential asset for production, it would be difficult for the rural poor to fulfil their basic needs within a reasonable period of time.

However, it is not enough to look at this problem only in terms of the government and the people. In addition to the importance of making clear the actions of government in a multilevel structure (i.e., central, regional and local), there is a need to clarify the distinction between two essential levels at which actions by the people themselves can be identified and carried out. These levels include the individual/household level and the collective/community level.

The attainment of basic human needs necessarily requires that each and every individual exerts his/her best efforts. This alone is not enough. The removal of crucial bottlenecks is often beyond the scope of individual or household efforts and requires collective effort by the people of the community concerned. A typical example is the distribution of water for irrigation. Without communitywide actions to construct distribution channels, the irrigation water in the main canal cannot be tapped. People should cooperate to ensure an equitable distribution of the water available. People should also be able to share maintenance labour in a fair manner. The same principles also apply to other aspects of life in the community. Communitywide actions are the prerequisites for meeting basic human needs.

Any concept or theory, to be meaningful, needs to be translated into effective policies, strategies, plans and actions. As such, while the fundamental philosophy underlying the concept of basic human needs is fairly clear, its interpretation into operational development policies and strategies can vary from one situation to another. At the same time, while the basic needs approach is understood by some as quite distinct from other approaches, such a distinction is so tenuous for others that it is just a matter of relative emphasis on certain essential dimensions of integrated development planning. Consequently no attempt is made in this volume to give a unified definition of the concept; rather, an attempt is made to exemplify many of the ways in which the concept has been developed, interpreted and applied.

ORGANIZATION

Chapter 2 of this volume: "Measurement of Basic Minimum Needs" by the United Nations Secretariat, is a detailed introduction to the concept of basic needs and the measurement of basic needs. It focuses on three aspects: (a) basic minimum needs as a planning concept, (b) information requirements for basic minimum needs, and (c) criteria for measuring minimum basic needs. It is my privilege to mention that this chapter was originally prepared by John Mathiason of the United Nations Secretariat for the Colloquium on the Methods of Planning for Comprehensive Regional Development held by UNCRD in October 1976 at Nagoya, and later made into an official paper of the United Nations. Chapter 3: "Basic Needs and Development Planning: Focus on India and the Philippines" jointly written by R. P. Misra and Ed. B. Prantilla, reviews the state of the art of policies and programmes related to the concept of basic human needs hitherto pursued in India and the Philippines. Chapter 4: "The Saemaul Movement and Concept of Basic Needs" by Sang-Chuel Choe reviews the well-known Saemaul Movement of Korea in the context of the task of meeting basic human needs, and indicates new directions in which the Saemaul Movement in the future may attain a new identity.

Chapter 5: "Planning for Children and Women in Regional Development" by Mujib R. Khan is devoted specifically to the problems of children and women in the development process. Chapter 6: "Local Level Planning: The Pakistan Experience" by Shoaib Sultan Khan and 7: "Innovation in the Health Delivery System: An Integrated Approach to Planning" by Ed. B. Prantilla and Aurora R. Pelayo are papers which add to empirical research findings of Chapters 4 and 8. Chapter 6 on Pakistan reports on the experience of a developing country in microlevel planning with an explicit focus on basic human needs. Chapter 7 presents experience with a health delivery system developed in one of the rural regions of the Philippines, and discusses its catalytic role in inducing an integrated local planning process. Chapter 8: "A Case Study of Basic Needs in Nepal" by Jiro Kawakita discusses the nature of basic needs identified in backward rural communities in Nepal facing the chronic threat of forest depletion, and advocates innovation in the perception and methodologies for needs-based development.

Chapter 9: "The Disenthronement of Basic Needs: Twenty Questions" by Benjamin Higgins, discusses extensively the concept of basic human needs from multifarious angles with special emphasis on its operational implications. The author explains how the basic needs approach differs from other approaches and discusses the implications of the difference for making the basic needs approach operational. Though critical as it might seem to the very concept of basic human needs, readers are reminded that a clear distinction should be made between the legitimate intentions and policy relevance of the concept on the one hand, and the imperfections and inconsistencies inherent in it — particularly in the context of operationalizing the concept of basic human needs, on the other. Development planning, because of the very nature of the development, must pursue various goals not necessarily compatible with each other. It is bound to be a highly complex exercise for which no one single concept or strategy, however rational or legitimate, can serve as panacea. The Higgins' chapter is expected to sharpen and deepen our insight into the complexities of development planning to which the concept of basic human needs should make a very meaningful contribution, be it enthroned or disenthroned.

The last chapter: "Studying the Basic Needs at the Microarea Level: A Methodological Note" by myself is a description in a nutshell of the concepts and methods employed in a research project on planning for basic needs at the microarea level conducted in India, Philippines and the Republic of Korea between 1977 and 1978. It also introduces the conclusion of the study as a whole. The bibliography attached at the end of the volume, while being selective, focuses on relevant experiences in Asia and the Pacific region.

2
MEASUREMENT OF BASIC MINIMUM NEEDS

UNITED NATIONS SECRETARIAT*

DEVELOPMENT STRATEGIES to meet basic needs of people have emerged recently as an alternative to the growth-oriented strategies which were originally proposed for the Second United Nations Development Decade. The realization that economic growth, even where achieved, does not necessarily lead to social justice and equity, has stimulated an international effort to define more effective strategies for the remainder of this decade and for the next.[1]

The adoption of a basic needs strategy will have implications for planning and planners. Planning based on growth could centre on the national level, the more dynamic sectors, and the criterion of economic efficiency; planning for basic needs requires a spatial focus, a focus on the less dynamic sectors and on target groups, and a criterion of equity in distribution. The latter approach requires planning for people rather than planning in the abstract.[2] Indeed, traditional planning tools and traditional types of information available to planners may be inadequate for basic needs strategies.

To determine what these basic needs are at a given time and place in planning, implementing, and assessment of the results of programmes to meet such needs is not easy. This paper seeks to examine many of the issues

---

* Centre for Social Development and Humanitarian Affairs of the Department of Economic and Social Affairs.

Revised version of a paper presented at the Colloquium on Methods of Planning for Comprehensive Regional Development, Nagoya, 25 October to 1 November 1976.

[1] International Labour Office, *Employment, Growth and Basic Needs: A One-World Problem; Report of the Director-General of ILO* (Geneva, 1976).

[2] Enrique Brown y Guillermo Geisse, "Planificación para los Planificadores o para el Cambio Social?" *Revista Latinoamericana de Estudios Urbanos Regionales* 3 (1973): 11–26.

involved in defining and measuring what have been termed by the United Nations Centre for Regional Development (UNCRD) as "basic needs."[3]

BASIC MINIMUM NEEDS AS A PLANNING CONCEPT

The premise for using basic minimum needs in planning is simple. Given a limited amount of resources to utilize for development, allocation of these resources should be such that the basic needs of the population are met. There is therefore a set of needs — and for each need a minimum level — which can be met within the limit of available resources. The goal of the planning exercise is to determine this set of basic minimum needs and to allocate resources so that the needs can be met.

There are three difficulties which are readily apparent: (1) the set of needs which *should* be met is greater than the set of needs which *can* be met, (2) the set of needs which can be defined by planners on technical grounds may differ from that perceived by the people, and (3) the set of needs which must be met in one situation may well differ from the set of needs which must be met in another.

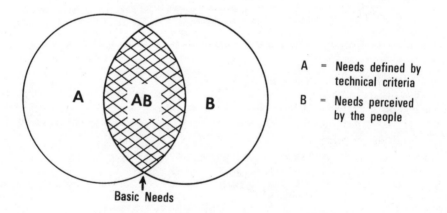

Figure 2-1. The Concept of Basic Needs

[3] United Nations Centre for Regional Development, *A Programme of Research: Improving the Method of Planning for Comprehensive Regional Development* (Nagoya, 1975).

To express the matter in logical terms, as in Figure 2-1, one could propose that, for every given area, there exists a set of needs which can be defined by technical criteria (A) and a set of needs which would be defined according to the perceptions of the people of the region (B). The two sets overlap and the conjoint set (AB) could be said to be the set of basic needs. For each need in that set, there can be said to be a minimum level which must be met to achieve satisfaction.

Operationalization of this concept of basic minimum needs is more difficult than to express it, since two types of needs are postulated: "objective" needs to be defined according to technical criteria and "subjective" needs to be defined according to popular perception.

"Objective" Needs

What is meant by a need? In common sense usage, needs are taken to mean requirements of some sort. Thus, the International Labour Office (ILO) defines basic needs in a broad way:

> First, they include certain minimum requirements of a family for private consumption: adequate food, shelter and clothing are obviously included, as would be certain household equipment and furniture. Second, they include essential services provided by and for the community at large, such as safe drinking water, sanitation, public transport, and health and education facilities.[4]

This type of need is defined normatively in general. Each society defines explicitly or implicitly norms about what levels of what things should exist in society. While there will be regional variations by level, the categories of needs given by the ILO are generally accepted. For many categories of needs, international standards have been set. Thus, a level of nutrition can be set as a standard, such as the minimum intake of 2,380 calories per head per day set by the Food and Agriculture Organization of the United Nations (FAO).[5] Similarly, a housing target can be set based on space available per person, such as the target of 5.25 square metres for Asia noted in ILO's study of basic needs.[6] These can be said to be basic needs in their respective areas. Standards have also been set for levels of services to be provided. In India, for example, the present Five Year Plan defines a national standard of one health centre per district and one subcentre for each taluka.

---

[4] ILO, *Employment, Growth and Basic Needs*, p. 8.

[5] Food and Agriculture Organization of the United Nations, *Provisional Indicative World Plan for Agricultural Development* (Rome, 1969).

[6] ILO, *Employment, Growth and Basic Needs*, p. 40.

While the standard chosen can be arbitrary, in many cases the minimum level defined is below that on which human beings can function normally. In terms of nutrition, when an individual falls below a certain level of caloric and protein intake, he will suffer physical damage. In those areas where resources are available only to meet the survivability minima, how to allocate resources is rather clear-cut: they must be allocated to achieve those minima as quickly and completely as possible. Thus, for example, planning for an area with chronic famine would centre on how to counter famine regardless of other possible needs which can be met.

Fortunately, most countries do not have permanent mass survival crises, although conditions may be far from adequate. This means that the levels of basic needs which must be met can be defined at some intermediate point between the survivability minimum and the optimum to be desired. When these levels are defined, they usually represent some norm such as "all children should go to school" and "everyone should have access to electricity" that are derived from a combination of what is already possible, given an appropriate allocation of resources, what the better portions of society already have, and what are internationally accepted norms for development. The specific needs and their levels will vary by country, and even by region within a country, although norms set are usually nationwide.

The range of needs which can be defined objectively is rather large and, to an extent, is bounded only by the limits of imagination. Once a society is beyond satisfaction of needs necessary for survival, some criterion must be applied in order to maintain a sense of perspective. Applied in many cases is the criterion of economic efficiency: the needs whose satisfaction leads to greater production and growth should be met first. An alternative is the needs perceived by the people.

"Subjective" Needs

For each society there is a set of needs perceived by the people that they feel should be satisfied as part of the development process. Planning based in part on the desires of the people for whom development is intended is now seen as necessary if plans are to be implemented, since this helps to ensure that opposition will not develop among the intended beneficiaries and will mobilize their active support — including their own resources — to assist in the effort being planned, and that the plan will reflect the realities of the area to be covered by it.[7] Indeed, community development has long emphasized

---

[7] United Nations, Department of Economic and Social Affairs, *Popular Participation in Decision Making for Development* (New York, 1975) (ST/ESA/31).

the necessity of using the "felt needs" of the population as the basis for promotion of self-help activities.[8] More recently, studies towards the "unified approach"to development planning have emphasized the need for popular participation as the means of achieving this unification between economic and social planning.[9] It could be argued that for every defined population there exists a set of needs the satisfaction of which at definable levels constitutes the minimum level of acceptability for development programmes. This might be seen as a societal "utility curve." Plotting this minimum needs curve could greatly assist in making realistic plans.

This concept of need has arisen out of studies on motivation. Social psychologists were among the first to use the concept, needs being seen as a principal element of the individual's cognitive structure. A need in this usage is something which is so strongly desired by an individual that it directs his behaviour. It is usually recognized that needs can be generated by physiological deprivation or by a positive desire to have something. It is also recognized that those needs generated by deprivation are atypical and that usually one of needs is based on attaining certain goals.

Psychologists have postulated the existence of a hierarchy of needs, ranging from basic physiological needs, such as food and shelter, to more complex cognitive satisfaction of needs for self-realization. Satisfaction of needs tends to progress up the hierarchy: as lower order needs are satisfied, higher order needs come to the fore.[10] Thus, needs which will be felt by people and the levels of attainment required to satisfy them will be constantly changing over time. In this subjective definition, needs are highly variable.

Needs also reflect the cultural and social conditions of a people. Thus, for example, in many societies religious fulfilment is a need considered by the people to be as food and shelter.

It should also be noted that the set of needs which are perceived will probably vary over time. Certain needs perceived in a time of famine will be different from those perceived in a time of plenty. Similarly, many needs may be a result of current fashions. As a society is more influenced by external communications, these perceived needs may become more volatile. Needs can also be altered through actions of leaders, who may succeed in creating or modifying peoples' perception of needs, particularly where the people have no clear perception of what their needs are.

---

[8] United Nations, Department of Economic and Social Affairs, *Popular Participation in Development: Emerging Trends in Community Development* (New York, 1971) (ST/SOA/106).

[9] United Nations, *Report on a Unified Approach to Development Analysis and Planning: Preliminary Report, of the Secretary-General* (New York, 1972) (E/CN.5/477).

[10] Abraham H. Maslow, "'Higher' and 'Lower' Needs," *Journal of Psychology* 25(1948): 433–36.

Conceptually, it is useful to distinguish in subjective needs those which are transitory and those which are held firmly. Concerning the latter the people have a set of cognitions which do not change over time. This can be said to consist of the basic needs perceived by the people. This distinction must be borne in mind in measuring needs.

Basic Minimum Needs

In practice, the categories of needs which can be defined by either an objective, normative approach or by a subjective, psychological approach tend to converge, at least, at the lower levels of needs. There is no doubt, for example, that there exist needs for food, shelter, clothing, education, and employment. Definition of nonmaterial needs, such as spiritual satisfaction and self-identity, might be more difficult, at least on a normative-objective basis.

The definition of categories of needs, whether suggested normatively or subjectively, is less difficult than finding in each case a numerical meaning for the terms "basic" and "minimum." Except for standards for certain basic types of needs, such as nutrition and shelter, where a level could be defined below which survival would be impossible, there are few readily apparent minima. Indeed, any other objective minimum standard would be arbitrary. Moreover, in areas such as education, where quality rather than quantity is more likely to be critical once the problem of distributing opportunities is overcome, setting standards is rather complex.

With regard to the needs felt by the people for whom planning is intended, the problem is that definitions both of "basic" and of "minimum" will be shifting. The set of needs which could be called "basic," where satisfaction is, in effect, indispensable, will change as needs are met and are replaced by new needs, also perceived as indispensable. Moreover, changed situations can themselves alter the set of needs, as when a technological innovation creates a new demand for itself. Similarly, minimum levels will change to the degree that achievement of one minimum level will force redefinition of a new, higher minimum level.

Methodologically, the only realistic compromise for defining basic minimum needs is to combine normative and objective criteria with subjective factors. For each planning exercise, basic needs would be defined by society. This is the minimum which is acceptable to the societal leadership. At the same time aggregated individual needs in this context would be defined as the collective preference among areas of need.

What would be measured in that set of needs determined objectively and normatively would be the existing levels of attainment, together with the expressed preferences of the population for action and among areas of activity. Basic minimum needs would be a construct of objective needs weighted by the popular preferences among them. Practically speaking, this means that the planners would have to define the areas in which public action would be expected. The present levels of attainment of these needs would have to be measured and the people polled on their priorities for action and desirable levels. Then a minimum level would have to be established for each need area, based on its relative priority among the people, popular desires, and, if possible; a normative standard. Thus, for example, if housing were an area of interest, the normative standard of 5.25 square metres could be established as a base, but if the popular desire were for a larger amount of space, the latter would become the minimum standard. And if, as opposed to other areas of possible activity, housing had a higher perceived importance, it would be defined as a basic need.

INFORMATION REQUIREMENTS FOR
BASIC MINIMUM NEEDS

Information is a raw material of the planner, forming the basis of his diagnosis, structuring his projections, and permitting him to evaluate the programmes which have been planned. The degree to which a planner will be able to plan in terms of basic minimum needs will depend on the degree to which he is able to obtain valid and reliable information about them.

As has been noted, basic minimum needs should be defined in area-specific and group-specific terms. This means the data on basic minimum needs also should be available on an area and group basis. In most countries, recent and reliable data on most basic minimum needs do not exist on an area or group basis.

Primary sources of data for planning purposes are national censuses, vital statistics collected as part of the civil registration process, and commercial accounts. These sources are designed to produce national statistics and national accounts. Consequently, coverage of many social indicators is rather restricted, although housing and occupational structure data are often available. Demographic statistics can also provide indicators of health and education levels. In fact, these types of statistics have been used up to now to develop national social indicators.[11]

[11] United Nations, Research Institute for Social Development, *Contents and Measurement of Socio-Economic Development: An Empirical Enquiry* (Geneva, 1970) (Report no. 70.10); United Nations, Statistical Office, *Towards a System of Social and Demographic Statistics* (New York, 1975) (Its

There are a number of critical limitations in the data usually used for planning purposes that reduce the data's usefulness in planning for basic minimum needs. The limitations in most countries are such that a new data base is probably required for basic minimum needs planning.

First, census and registration data are incomplete in terms of measuring objective needs. Information is usually available on family size, monetary income, general mortality and morbidity, housing, and education levels. Continuous data are usually not available about nutrition (unless a special study has been undertaken), use of health facilities, group participation, and patterns of saving and consumption. Even if the data are collected, the coverage, in many countries is poor, particularly if the source is registration data. In one Asian country, for example, systematic collection of vital statistics stopped when local government units charged with civil registration were abolished. Thus, data on death causes were available only in urban hospitals, with planners unable to ascertain prevailing patterns of diseases in·rural areas or urban slums.

Second, very few countries collect data on subjective needs. Indeed, only a few developing countries, such as India and Thailand, have household sample survey organizations. No country systematically obtains information on popular desires as part of the governmental information collection process, although this type of information on a national basis is collected by private polling organizations in a number of industrialized countries.

Third, available data do not usually reflect spatial aspects of development. Census figures, for example, are usually not broken down by region, except for demographic figures. Moreover, those that are presented in subnational series usually appear considerably late in the process of publication, and may' not be classified according to planning areas.

Over the long run, it may be possible to institutionalize systems of statistics which provide necessary information for basic minimum needs planning. The United Nations has suggested standards for social and demographic statistics which could fill some of the existing gaps.[12] In the context of the ILO's concern with basic needs, the concept of a social accounting matrix to organize planning data has been suggested.[13] However, until these systems have wide application in developing countries, with data series based on

studies in methods; F, no. 18) (ST/ESA/STAT/SER.F/18); Ray Horn, "Social Indicators for Development Planning and Analysis," *International Labour Review* III (June 1975): 483–506; Nancy Bastar, ed., *Measuring Development* (London: Frank Cass, 1972). [See especially the articles by Donald McGranahan and by Irma Adelman and Cynthia Taft Morris.]

[12] United Nations, Statistical Office, *Towards a System of Social and Demographic Statistics.*

[13] Graham Pyatt and Erik Thorbecke, *Planning Techniques for a Better Future: A Summary of a Research Project on Planning for Growth, Redistribution, and Employment* (Geneva: ILO, 1976).

planning regions, there appears to be no alternative to undertaking the collection of new data as an integral part of the subnational planning process.

Planners customarily resist acquiring new data as part of the initial planning process. Based on past experiences, it is often felt that obtaining new data is too expensive in monetary terms, takes too much time, and thereby would delay the production of a plan and, even might yield too much information to be useful. These legitimate concerns, however, must be conditioned by another set of factors. First, the cost of planning without adequate data may be higher than the cost of collecting data. Second, with few exceptions, such as preparation of emergency plans, the planning process itself extends over time so that data acquisition over a period of six months should not significantly retard the planning process. Third, whether or not new data are acquired during the diagnosis period, it must be acquired subsequently if the impact of development programmes generated by the planning process is to be assessed.

In determining whether the cost of obtaining new data outweighs the cost of planning without adequate data, some consideration should be given to the fact that the cost of data acquisition is related directly to the total volume and precision required of the data. For example, censuses are almost completely precise, since data are collected from every individual in the society. There is, at the point of collection, no error. Moreover, the volume of data collected in censuses is very large. Thus, the cost of executing national censuses is very high and much time is required to process and analyse the data. In contrast, sample surveys are used to estimate conditions in populations with data collected from only a small proportion of the population. While the precision is somewhat less than that of a census, the cost is similarly small.[14]

It can be argued that planners do not always require census-level precision to make effective decisions. What is required is information which allows the planner to allocate resources spatially with a reasonable assurance that he is not making major errors. In terms of planning for basic minimum needs, the planner would require an indication of a rough structure of needs, both subjective and objective, as they are distributed in space and among groups. The data would have to be used subsequently to determine whether the needs had been met and the programmes resulting from the planning process had had their desired impact on their intended beneficiaries.

[14] Of course, national censuses are undertaken for purposes other than planning and the data generated by them are usually available for planners at little or no cost. But if the cost of the national census were added to the cost of planning, the total would be very high.

Measurement of basic minimum needs should be seen in the context of obtaining new data in a cost-effective manner as part of the planning process itself. Concrete discussion on how to do this is based on a number of examples of information systems which were developed to measure the impact of development programmes on their beneficiaries. These included an evaluation of the Brazilian extension system, [15] evaluation of a river basin development project, [16] planning of a rural development programme in regions in four Latin American countries, designing for monitoring and evaluation of a land settlement programme in a Middle Eastern country, and designing for a rural development information system in a South Asian country.[17]

Practical experience, it should be noted, does not come from planning based explicitly on basic minimum needs. Few countries have yet adopted this approach, particularly in regional planning. However, the information systems which were utilized are compatible with the requirements of a basic minimum needs strategy. Moreover, in each case, data acquisition did not require more than one to six months, depending on the volume of data.

Measuring "basic minimum needs" is a matter of measuring levels of basic needs as defined by planners based on externally provided standards and then analysing them in the context of subjective preferences of the population. The process of determining criteria for measurement can follow the pattern common to all questions of scientific measurement. These include:

(a) What will be measured? This means defining the concept of needs.

(b) Where will it be measured? The locus of measurement must be defined in terms of a universe, sampling units, and sampling methods.

(c) How will it be measured? Methodology of data collection must be indicated.

---

[15] Associacão Brasileira de Crédito e Assistência Rural, *Availiacão dos Trabalhos nos Projectos de Bem-Estar: Plano Basico da Availiacao* (Rio de Janeiro, 1973).

[16] Centro Nacional de Capacitación e Investigation Aplicada para el Desarrollo Regional y Local, *El Modelo PREB/CIADEC para la Evaluación de un Pequeño Proyecto de Desarrollo* (Maracay, 1973).

[17] The methodological aspects of the other information systems have not yet been published. Much of the subsequent discussion is based on unpublished material.

CRITERIA FOR MEASURING BASIC MINIMUM NEEDS

What to Measure

For objective needs, the measurement problem is less than for subjective needs. Objective types of need of interest must be defined by the planners, based on observation of the region and study of its problems. Usually needs can be said to fall into three broad categories: levels of living, factors of population, and services.

Levels of living refer basically to the physical condition of a person. Thus, they usually are measured by the presence or absence of certain goods and amenities. In some cases, an index is created according to whether an individual has a good house, potable water, certain types of furniture, and sanitation services. As an alternative, more complete data on housing can reflect a wider range of needs. In Venezuela and other Latin American countries, types of houses were used as a comprehensive indicator, since it was usually associated with the presence of other amenities.

Nutrition is an important area of need. Measurement of levels of nutrition is a field in which a great deal of efforts has been made, usually in the context of special nutrition surveys.[18] However, since information gathering for basic minimum needs cannot be based on a comprehensive examination of each need area, the approach taken in Brazil was to collect two rather less precise types of data which would give a reasonable indication of the level of nutrition in the population. Nutrition is based on both quantity of food and dietary balance. It was felt that people with a balanced diet would generally have a sufficient quantity of food and that therefore measuring the degree to which the average diet was balanced would give an adequate indication of the general level of nutrition. Families in a sample were asked about the frequency with which foods from specific critical food groups were consumed. In addition, families were asked to tell what they had eaten in their meals during the previous twenty-four hours. Putting these two pieces of information together, it would be possible to determine the degree of balance in the diet and from that to infer the level of nutrition.

For physical health, needs were measured in one Latin American country through studying the prevalence of infant mortality and the frequency of

---

[18] Michael C. Latham, *Planning and Evaluation of Applied Nutrition Programmes* (Rome: Food and Agricultural Organization of the United Nations, 1972) (FAO Nutritional series, no. 26).

illness. It was assumed that low levels of health in a family would be associated with a higher than average infant mortality, measured as the percentage of children born to a family who died within the first six years, and a
higher frequency of illness, measured by the number of days during the previous six months the mother or father had been ill. These two figures gave a
reasonable approximation of levels of physical well-being for planning
purposes.

A second need area could be called "factors of production." While
needs are often seen as exclusively social in nature, in practice there are economic needs as well. These range from a need for employment to needs for
factors of productive inputs and infrastructure. The principal measure of
need in this sense is probably net income, reflecting the overall return realized from productive effort. In most of the data cases to which reference has
been made, the method of obtaining income was through a reconstruction of
the previous economic year. This was especially necessary for farmers, much
of whose income was not monetized (such as food produced for home consumption or sold through barter arrangements). The amount of detailed
information which was required in this procedure was rather large, since it
involved calculation not only of the value of the product but also of the costs
of production. Such detail could be justified since it also provided data on the
structure of production which was necessary for micro planning. The general
procedure was to ask crop by crop or product by product:

(a) How much was produced?
(b) How much was sold and at what price?
(c) How much did each productive input (ranging from seed and
    fertilizer through hired labour) cost?
(d) How many work-days did the person and family members them-
    selves provide?

The exercise also permitted description, in the case of farmers, of the
levels of factors of production, including amount of arable land, use of modern inputs (fertilizer, insecticides, certified seeds), and reliance on hired
labour. Additionally, acceptable data were obtained on levels of employment. In one case in Venezuela it was found, for example, that the average
farmer was working only half time, thus indicating the degree of disguised
unemployment.

In general, the degree to which "factors of production" needs are measured may depend on whether government policy considers the income-
generating activities of the population to represent a need. Clearly, however,
a development strategy based on an overall principle of distributive justice
would consider them a major area of concern.

Measurement of service needs is relatively straightforward. What is observed first is availability (Does the service exist in the area?), then access (Can the beneficiaries use the facility?), and finally use (Do the beneficiaries actually use the service?). In practice, the indicators tend to be based on availability (such as doctors per 1,000 population) rather than on use, which is a more appropriate measure; but in some cases a more complex measure based on a combination of availability, access, and use is prepared.

In one Latin American country, level of need for medical services was measured by determining whether a health centre was within one-hour walking distance, whether it was constantly staffed, and, by asking a sample of individuals about how many families used the centre. However, in order to assure that a high level of use of the health centre did not, in fact, reflect an unfavourable health situation, the measure of use was modified to include the percentage of use for preventive rather than curative treatment. Need was deemed to be higher where there was (1) no health centre, (2) a centre existed but was not constantly staffed, or (3) centre users formed a low percentage of the population and (4) use was mainly for curative rather than preventive treatment.

Qualitative objective indicators are less common. By this is meant indicators of the quality of institutions of interest. There is, however, a common sense approach which can be followed, as long as data are aggregated by community. For each institution, such as hospitals, schools, credit banks, and the like which affect a basic minimum need area, it is possible to make a qualitative rating based on a number of dimensions:

(a) What proportion of the intended beneficiary population for the institution actually use the institution?

(b) What proportion of the staff positions are filled? What proportion of staff meet minimum national standards?

(c) How close does the physical plant approximate the national optimum?

(d) Where national norms exist, to what extent do beneficiaries achieve national norms after using the institution (for such activities as educational attainment, health, or creditworthiness)?

Indicators can be constructed for each institution of interest to the planner.

Measurement of subjective needs or preference is less common. However, there are now examples of use of subjective measure of job satisfaction as a part of employment studies, [19] as well as in the development of

[19] Ray Horn, "Social Indicators," pp. 488–89.

more refined measures of economic welfare.[20] Determination of subjective preferences has long been an aspect of "motivation research" in advertising. Thus, a certain experience has been accumulated, although this type of measure has not often been used for planning, especially in developing countries. Common sense suggests that subjective needs will vary considerably over time and among places, so that measurement will have to make allowances for this.

A simple approach would be to ask a sample of people what they think they need. Replies however may not be particularly stable: in a drought, the perceived need tends to be for water: if the next day there is a cloudburst, the perceived need may well be for flood control. Public opinion researchers have frequently noted that, because situational factors have strong influences on opinions, the expressions of people in simple opinion polls and attitude surveys have tended to be poor predictors of behaviour.[21]

Measuring of preferences usually takes the form of asking people to either (1) select preferred items from a longer list or (2) make paired comparisons. In the latter, two alternatives, A and B, are presented in the form "Do you prefer A or do you prefer B?" (Or, "Is A a greater need or is B a greater need?") Then, A and B each are compared with C. In theory, it should be possible to establish an order of preference, due to a presumed intransitivity in the relationship, such as A>B and B>C then A>C. Unfortunately, in a reasonably large number of cases, this type of relationship has been found not to be intransitive and the phenomenon can be observed that an individual may prefer A to B and B to C, but also prefer C to A. It is suspected that one reason for this is that the alternatives specified in the question may stimulate the respondent to an answer which he would not have otherwise made. Thus, for example, a respondent may never have considered comparing A and C, and the question which poses the comparison may suggest it for the first time. The problem that the question itself may suggest a preference may help to explain why responses to "forced-choice questions" are so poorly related to behaviour.

Forced-choice questioning has a further disadvantage in that the depth of interest about a given alternative as well as the degree of information held about it, all of which are important in determining whether an individual's

[20] Burkhard Strumpel, ed., *Economic Means for Human Needs: Social Indicators of Well-Being and Discontent* (Ann Arbor: Survey Research Center, Institute for Social Research, University of Michigan, 1976).

[21] Milton Rokeach, "Attitude Change and Behavior Change," *Public Opinion Quarterly* 30 (1966): 529–50; Leon Festinger, "Behavioral Support for Opinion Change," *Public Opinion Quarterly* 28 (1964): 404–17.

concern will be translated into behaviour, cannot be ascertained. What can be learned is that some of a set of posed alternatives are preferred in general, but not the nature of that preference.

To avoid intrusive questions which themselves suggest answers, some researchers then explore the respondents' ability to think about fundamental conditions. This method has been used in a number of studies in different countries, including Brazil, Colombia, Mexico, Panama, and Venezuela.[22] The procedure is to first ask, "What are the principal problems facing this community?" This identifies the universe of problems perceived by a respondent at any given time. And, since needs can be expressed as "problems," it represents his most perceived need. If more than one problem is named, the sequence then follows with, "Of these, which is the most important?" This identifies the most salient need, as perceived by the respondent. Then, a sequence of questions about this problem is asked, including "What do you think is the cause of this problem?" and "What do you feel are the possible solutions for this problem?" Since these latter questions are problem specific, it is not feasible to deal with their contents. Rather, the sequence has been coded in order to establish the degree to which the individual has "thought through" the problem. It is felt that a problem for which an individual can specify both cause and potential solution is one which is more "firm" than one about which an individual has not developed a set of cognitions. A feeling of personal powerlessness has been found to be closely related to the degree to which an individual is unable to fully define his most strongly felt problem.[23]

Using this set of questions for each community, it is possible to identify that group of needs (expressed as problems) felt by a substantial portion of the people living in the community. It is also possible to determine which of these has been cognitively developed and therefore is likely to provoke behaviour.

An example of the results obtained by this procedure can be found in one study involved in the planning for Ciudad Guayana, a new city in Venezuela. The application of the problem-solving sequence to a sample of lower-income residents found that the subjective needs were as given in Table 2-1.

[22] See, for example, John R. Mathiason, "Patterns of Powerlessness Among Urban Poor: Towards the Use of Mass Communications for Rapid Social Change," *Studies in Comparative International Development* 7(1972): 64—84.

[23] Ibid., pp. 75—76.

Table 2-1. Perceived Problems in Ciudad Guayana

Problem	Per cent of residents (n = 400)	Per cent of residents having opinion (n = 304)
1. Lack of running water or sewers	28.7	37.8
2. Lack of pavement or street repairs	19.8	26.0
3. Inadequate garbage collection	8.0	10.5
4. Public order problems	8.0	10.5
5. Lack of various other public services*	10.7	14.3
6. Personal problems	0.5	0
	75.7	100.0

*Lack of housing, telephones, electricity, etc. None greater than 5 per cent.

The perceived needs clustered around the two items of community services and infrastructure. The need receiving the highest number of mentions was usually characterized by having been thought through as indicated by clear definition. It should be noted, however, that the priority reflected in the popular perceptions detected in the sample survey differed from those seen by the planners and, in fact, the conflict in priorities had already produced some problems between the planners and residents of the city.

Where to Measure

It would seem that the answer to the question, "Where should we measure needs?" is rather simple: needs must be observed at the individual level and aggregated. Most existing social indicators are of this type such as measurement of education by an average number of years of study or percentage of children in a given age group who are in school. Clearly the individual is, ultimately, the focus of development. It is thus sensible to collect data from individuals and aggregate the responses as averages or other descriptors of a given distribution. Vital registration statistics, censuses, and national sample surveys are usually conducted and analysed on this basis.

Given that it is possible to construct a new regional data base with special surveys, it is worthwhile considering whether the standard method of collecting data from such surveys — individual interviews aggregated to produce group information — is the best method to assess basic minimum needs. For comprehensive planning, the spatial dimension is critical. But standard surveys, when analysed, tend to produce data not easily divisible into area data. Analysis is typically based on artificially defined analytical groups whose composition is as much determined by the number of data sets available (number of interviews) as by information requirements. Except for data on large urban areas, data sets for given localities are often too small to provide much useful analytical data about any locality, particularly in terms of indices where two or more variables must be combined. To provide sufficient data using customary techniques would dramatically require increasing sample sizes, with and accompanying increase in cost.

More importantly, however, standard individual-based surveys lack information on the critical "community" variable. A community can be defined as a spatial variable encompassing that number of people who can interact with each other consistently on a face-to-face basis. The size, in this case, can vary from a small village to a section of a city, depending on the pattern of interactions. The community is the location of a number of important nonindividual factors required for planning. These include local voluntary organizations, leadership patterns, distribution of services and their quality (such as education and health), and such physical environmental variables as transportation and communication infrastructure. The importance of community and other locational variables in establishing social indicators for local and intermediate levels has been underscored by recent work of the United Nations Research Institute for Social Development (UNRISD).[24]

To measure basic minimum needs, the community variable is important for a number of reasons. First, in determining existing levels for need categories such as education, health, and other aspects where remedies are provided through government services, it is possible to estimate the quality of the service at the community level. Second, and more important, data on voluntary organizations and leadership can include information on group preferences. For the planner concerned with acceptability of a plan, the preferences expressed by organized groups and leaders may be more important than the sum of average preferences of individuals. This is because in expressed group preferences, the effect of local political power is already taken into account, whereas an average of individual preferences may not represent this. Whether or not a preference is firm enough to lead to action depends on a number of factors, including the salience of the issue (how strongly it is felt) and the degree of understanding involved. Individuals with preferences may hold them weakly or with little understanding, whereas

[24] UNRISD, *The Measurement of Real Progress at the Local Level* (Geneva, 1973) (Report no. 73.3).

when an issue reaches the level of an expressed group preference, the salience and understanding of an issue tend to be present. Moreover, it is clear that the relatively more powerful in any group tend to lead others and that the leaders' preference is therefore likely to be more significant than that of the followers. This type of weighting is, of course, lost in preferences estimated by an average of individual responses.

Using the type of questions on problems used to measure subjective needs, it is possible to ascertain those needs perceived by community leaders, as well as formally recognized by organizations. Obtaining this information requires interviewing community leaders and, if possible, requesting the information through meetings with the organizations. This latter practice was done in Venezuela.[25]

It is quite possible that there will be a discrepancy between preferences expressed by organized groups and those expressed by individuals. If so, this is in itself an important indicator of possible political conflict within the communities, that can assist the planner in determining precisely which needs are basic. Indeed, where a discrepancy exists, there is a possibility of a change in preferences as individual preferences either change those of organized groups or are moulded through the process of participation.

In order to ensure that preferences are adequately weighted for power factors and provide essential spatial data for the analysis of basic minimum needs, a model based on data collection and analysis at the community level has been developed and applied in a number of countries, including those previously identified. In the approach taken in these countries, the population to be surveyed is defined in terms of communities, which are then to be classified (or stratified, in technical terminology) into types according to the dominant characteristics of the region. A sample of communities is then taken, which is sufficiently large to assure that all major types of communities in the region are represented. Each community is then studied, both through small-scale individual surveys and through in-depth interviewing. Individual responses are aggregated to the community level and the data are used to further describe the communities. The community data are then aggregated to provide a regional profile of communities. This "system of community case studies" has been used as a basis for continued collection of data on the progress of development through systematic restudies of the communities.

[25] Centro Nacional de Capacitación Aplicada para el Desarrollo Regional y Local, *Estudio Socio-Economico del Asentamento Caicara* (Maracay, 1973).

How to Measure

The method of a system of case studies was adopted in order to obtain new data on needs in the countries noted earlier in response to the question of how to measure in such a way that data are available at a relatively low cost, with generalization possible according to spatial distribution in an area, and that a basis for subsequent data collection is assured. A sample of communities in a region is required in order to reduce cost. The samples chosen are based on a stratification method which ensures that the communities selected will be a representative sample of the types of communities existing in the region. In this sampling the concern is to have as large a number of different communities as resources permit. Within each community a rather small sample of individuals is taken, also stratified to maximize the representativeness of the sample. However, the precision of the individual-level sample in each community is not very high. The reasoning behind this approach to sampling is that, for planning purposes, the degree of precision required at the community level is much higher than at the individual level and, in effect, there will be little direct aggregation of the individual data at the regional level.

In a state in Mexico, it was found that major cultural factors of language and religion, as well as factors of modernization, were reflected according to established subdistricts. A sample of thirty communities was drawn from ten groups of subdistricts. A subsequent check on the reliability of the sample found that it permitted estimation of a known factor within 5 per cent. This meant that planners could be reasonably assured that the average taken from the sample was probably within about 5 per cent of the true value in the entire population.

The procedure followed, once the system of case studies was defined, was to collect data on needs, as well as on other programmatic factors, in each of the communities. This was done by sending in teams of interviewers to obtain information from interviews with families, with leaders, or with government officials, according to the type of data required. It was found that a team of five interviewers, usually drawn out of planning units, training institutions, or line agencies, could completely cover a community in three days. Thirty communities would require therefore about ninety working days for a team of five, or thirty working days for three teams.

To avoid the problem of delays in having data available due to tabulation at a central place, in a number of countries tabulation was made by field teams after each community was surveyed, so that only thirty sets of data had to be added up to provide regional totals. In one country, it was decided to process the information on a computer, but software problems led ultimately to a delay in data tabulation.

As an end result of this processing, information is obtained which can provide a profile of the communities in a given region; this consists of four types of data which can be used to identify basic minimum needs:

(a) data on the average magnitude and rough distribution (quartiles, for example) by community of objective needs measured at the individual level. For example, one could assert, as was done in a diagnostic evaluation for planning a rural development programme in one country, that the mean yearly net family income in the lowest quarter of the communities was equivalent to US$50, the mean in the highest quarter was US$405, and in the median community it was US$200. Or, alternatively, the percentage of families who never visit a health centre in the median community is 10 per cent with a range from 90 per cent in the lowest community to 0 per cent in the highest community;

(b) data on the magnitude and rough distribution according to communities of objective needs measured at the community level. For example, data are obtained which indicate that the number of kilometres of paved road in the median community is X, ranging from Y in the lowest to Z in the highest;

(c) data on the average needs perceived by residents in communities based on individual-level interviews. For example, one could develop statements such as, in X per cent of the communities the main problem perceived individually is potable water;

(d) data on the needs perceived collectively (as expressed by leaders and organizations) by the communities in the region. For example, it would be possible to assert that "improved housing" is considered to be a major problem in X per cent of the communities.

The four data sets can be further analysed in order to establish (1) the set of basic minimum needs, (2) spatial distribution of minimum needs, and (3) the relationship among needs as seen objectively and subjectively. If it is assumed that basic minimum needs are perceived externally and by the recipient people, it is possible to classify needs into a hierarchy.

The most fundamental needs, perceived as objectively requiring attention, are perceived as needs in most of the communities by individuals and also perceived as needs by organizations. These could be defined as those needs which clearly require major allocations of available resources.

Two intermediate categories can also be identified. First those needs which are identified as critical by external observers but which are not perceived either by individuals or by organizations but are noticeable by both.

This constitutes a set of needs for which perception can be created within the region, since it is already present passively. A second set of needs is those which are not perceived to be objectively necessary but are perceived by both individuals and their organizations to be important. This constitutes a type of need that probably has to be met regardless of its economic importance. Cases in which popular perceptions lead to programmes of investment in churches or temples in order to alleviate a perceived nonmaterial, higher-level need are examples of this.

Finally, there exist those classes of needs which are seen by only one of the three types of observer. These constitute a reservoir of areas for action or, if the objective case can be made, those areas where a special effort would have to be made to create a popular perception of needs before the programme could be implemented.

FURTHER WORK ON DATA ACQUISITION METHODS

The method of data acquisition described above for measuring basic minimum needs has been found useful in a number of countries with different information requirements. It would, however, not be proper to suggest that this approach represents the only way to measure basic minimum needs. Other methods, including those based on establishing regional information sytems within the context of routine data gathering through census, vital registration, and sample surveys, may be applicable, particularly where time and financial constraints are less stringent. Experience to date do suggest several firm criteria for data acquisition, which would be applicable regardless of method:

(a) Data should be acquired based on some kind of spatial stratification to assure that the places where felt needs exist can be identified with reasonable accuracy;

(b) Data obtained from individuals should be aggregated at the community level to permit a spatial profile and their integration with other community-level data;

(c) The data acquired should be designed to be compatible with future data requirements so that, as a minimum, it will be possible to show whether the needs identified in the planning process have been met.

There is, in addition to these criteria, a possibility that there has been far more acceptance of the notion that popular participation in planning is useful for development than there has been elaboration of means by which this can be achieved. One lesson of the method discussed here is that the process of data acquisition through a system of community case studies implies a form of popular participation. This method may, in itself, serve as a vehicle for stimulating greater popular participation, since the key to participation in planning is that the planners genuinely know what are the people's needs and priorities. Planning based on obtaining information on basic minimum needs may, with little difficulty, provide the basis for a broad-based popular involvement in the planning process.

3

BASIC NEEDS AND DEVELOPMENT PLANNING: FOCUS ON INDIA AND THE PHILIPPINES

R. P. MISRA AND ED. B. PRANTILLA

INTRODUCTION

UNTIL RECENTLY, development was coterminous with economic growth — the rate at which the gross domestic product of a country increases. It was a derivative of massive investment in farms and factories, and in modern technology. Industrialization, urbanization, and Westernization often termed "modernization" signalled the arrival of development. To usher in this great "divinity" people must work hard; they must change the style of their life; in short, they must transform themselves to receive development. The material welfare of people was implicit in the very process of development; it did not need elaborate strategies and policies. And once the material welfare was accomplished, everyone must be happy. There would be ups and downs here and there, but the market forces would be able to even them out; so went the reasoning.

The above reasoning had empirical bases too. Economic development of Western nations during the nineteenth and twentieth centuries had followed these same paths and patterns. Of course the conditions then were different. These countries had the resources of almost the whole world at their disposal. And the goods produced by them had captive markets — again all over the world. It was argued that the problem of resources could be resolved by foreign aid, and the question of markets by the free market economy or by linking it to one of the two power-blocks — the US-dominated Western block, and the USSR-dominated Eastern block.

This euphoria about development lasted until about the end of the 1950s. The new nations which had just emerged from colonial suppression of many decades saw in development, not only a hope for survival, but survival itself. Country after country launched national development plans — annual plans, five-year plans, ten-year plans, and long-term perspective plans. Foreign aid started flowing slowly but steadily especially to countries which fitted into the scheme of things envisaged by the developed countries. To start with, political leanings and affiliations were the major factors determining the amount, content, and terms of aid. But as the years rolled on and the cold war between the two power blocks intensified, ideology gave way to military alliance, and economic aid gave way to military aid. The security of a developing country was no more seen in its economic and social strength; it was seen in military alliances. Many developing countries fell prey to this new notion of national development. Sophisticated military hardwares were available for the asking if only a strategically placed developing country would fall in line with the concept of mutual security, wherein "mutuality" meant nothing more than the interests of the aid-giving country.

The late fifties and the whole of sixties saw the proliferation of military alliances, military bases and military aid. Economic aid receded in the background. It did not decrease in absolute terms but it grew only at a snail's pace and did not even touch the top of the iceberg of poverty and pestilence which afflicted the developing countries. Whatever little aid did flow, was tied to projects which could not be launched unless the expertise and equipment needed were purchased in the donor country at a price fixed by the donor.

Bilateral aid without strings attached became uncommon, if not rare. Fortunately, however, the United Nations activities in the field of development expanded rather rapidly, thanks to the growing membership of the UN, accounted for by the developing countries. Organizations like United Nations Development Programme (UNDP), United Nations International Children's Emergency Fund (UNICEF) and the World Bank expanded their developmental roles. This did compensate partially for the offending disinterest of the developed countries to assist the developing countries.

By the end of the 1960s, a few things were obvious enough to make anyone interested in the developing countries sit up and think of alternative ways of looking at development. The first was the growing reluctance of the developed countries to massively assist the developing countries except on terms and conditions which a self-respecting nation could not accept. Secondly, perhaps because of the very contradictions of the post-Second World War period, ideology was no more the moving force behind national alliances — it gave place to national interest which, when translated in real terms, meant perpetuation, if not further strengthening of the international order rooted in the colonial past. Thirdly, not many countries had achieved high enough rates of economic growth to make any perceptible impact on the well-being of the poor majority, except under very special circumstances such as abundance of natural resources, or massive flow of capital from outside for extra-developmental reasons. And fourthly, despite spectacular achievements of at least some developing countries (spectacular when seen in the light of the odds against them), and the not-too-bad performance of others, the lot of the poor who constituted the majority in most developing countries, did not improve at the rate the economy grew. In many countries, the gap between the few rich and many poor further widened and the number of poor in absolute terms increased as the new opportunities created by new development naturally went to those who were better qualified to benefit from them. While the future of the country was being shaped by international forces, that of the poor was being determined by the market forces, and while the development of the national economies was slow, that of the people was slower and at times even regressive.

A number of studies in the early seventies pointed to continuing deplorable living conditions of the poor majority in the developing countries. Starting with the World Employment Conference in 1976, International Labour Office (ILO) studies in a number of countries pointed to the same conclusions and gave rise to what is now called the Basic Needs approach to development. The reasons why economic growth did not benefit the poor were many and perhaps they worked in conjunction with each other. But these studies found the culprit in the style of development followed by the developing countries. The blame was squarely put on the Western model of development, on the overemphasis on growth, on the neglect of distributive justice, on low priority for employment and basic needs of the people, especially the poor. The argument was that development had no meaning if it did not improve the quality of life of the people, if it did not eradicate poverty, and if it failed to benefit those who were deprived of even the basic needs of life.

It is now clear that more than a decade of rapid growth in underdeveloped countries has been of little or no benefit to perhaps a third of their population. Although the average per capita income of the Third World has increased by 50 per cent since 1960, this growth has been very unequally distributed among countries, regions within countries, and socioeconomic groups.[1]

As expressed by the world economists meeting at Cocoyoc:

> Our first concern is to redefine the whole purpose of development. This should not be to develop thing but to develop man. Human beings have basic needs — food, shelter, clothing, health, education. Any process of growth that does not lead to their fulfilment — or, even worse, disrupts them — is a travesty of the idea

---

[1] Hollis Chenery et al., *Redistribution with Growth: Policies to Improve Income Distribution in Developing Countries in the Context of Economic Growth* (London: Oxford University Press, 1974).

of development. A growth process that benefits only the wealthiest minority and maintains or even increases the disparities between and within countries is not development. It is exploitation.[2]

. . . each human being, simply because of his existence, has in- alienable rights regarding the satisfaction of basic needs — nutri- tion, housing, health, education — that are essential for complete and active incorporation into his culture. These needs are taken to be basic because, unless each one of them is satisfied, it is impossible to participate actively and with dignity in the human university. These needs are invariable in that they are common to all members of the special species regardless of culture, origin, race, sex, etc.[3]

The perspective on development should be founded on four basic principles:

First, the basic problem of development should be redefined as a selective attack on the worst form of poverty. Second . . . con- sumption planning should move to the centre of the stage; produc- tion planning should be geared to it. . . . Third, the concern for more production and better distribution should be brought together. . . . Fourth, and this is implicit in the third, employment should become a primary objective.[4]

All these are fine and well said. In fact, if one reads the writing of statesmen and national leaders like Nehru, Mao, Nyerere and many others, they had said these long before this ''new'' awareness about the poor and their needs. Something went wrong somewhere and Basic Needs did not get the priority they ought to have. But the new findings did not stop at re- emphasizing the Basic Needs components in national planning. They became the bases for enunciating the so-called Basic Needs approach to development. The approach got some adherents to begin with, but soon it became a controversial matter. Its original authors claim that much of what now goes in the name of Basic Needs approach to development, is not what they had conceived; it is something which has been advanced by those who jumped on the bandwagon later.

Whatever the case may be, the Basic Needs approach continues to be an important element of a new style of development now in the process of discussion and debates. It is, therefore, important that we should understand the theoretical as well as empirical bases of this approach lest it becomes yet another fad to be discarded unceremoniously in due course of time.

[2] ''Cocoyoc Declaration,'' *Development Dialogue* No. 2 (1974): 88—96
[3] Amilcar O. Herrera et al., *Catastrophe or New Society? A Latin American World Model* (Ottawa: International Development Research Centre, 1976).
[4] Mahbub ul Haq, *The Poverty Curtain: Choices for the Third World* (New York: Columbia Univer- sity Press, 1976), p. 35.

THE CONCEPT OF BASIC NEEDS

The concept of basic needs has been looked upon favourably by many practitioners of development planning as a means to make development more relevant and responsive to the needs of the people. The usefulness of the concept is beyond question. However, a number of issues relating to the operationalization of the concept have come to fore. To date, the problems remain unsettled. One of these problems relates to the definition of what constitutes the basic needs.

The definition of basic needs varies widely because the needs as such ". . . vary from person to person, from time to time, from culture to culture, from farm to farm, from city to city, from country to country."[5] It is, however, agreed that there is no such problem when we are considering the needs of the poor. They are deprived of certain goods, services, and opportunities essential for decent life no matter how one defines the term "decent."

On the other hand, the ILO definition of basic needs includes "the fulfilment of basic human rights which are not only ends in themselves but also contribute to the attainment of other goals."[6] While others consider freedom, human rights, etc., beyond the scope of those basic needs which should be met universally, irrespective of the degree of freedom people may enjoy.[7] They distinguish the basic material needs like food, shelter, clothing, etc., from ethical absolutes, like freedom, human rights, popular participation, etc.

If we accept basic needs to be "those threshold needs, mainly biophysical which must be met, to maintain survival,"[8] then we are conceptually living in the medieval times when wages were kept at a survival level. The bare necessities enumerated usually include food, clothing, shelter, health, safe drinking water, and education.[9] In other words, our emphasis is on meeting the consumption needs; and on the consequence rather than the cause of poverty. In such a definition, the forces and situations which bring about the lack of food, shelter, clothing, etc., do not find a pivotal place.

[5] Harlan Cleveland, "Introduction: Toward an International Poverty Line" in John McHale and Magda C. McHale, *Basic Human Needs: A Framework for Action.* (New Brunswick, N.J.: Transaction Books, 1978).
[6] International Labour Office, *Employment, Growth and Basic Needs: A One World Problem* (New York: Praeger, 1977).
[7] International Labour Office, *Meeting Basic Needs: Strategies for Eradicating Mass Poverty and Employment* (Geneva; 1977).
[8] McHale and McHale, *Basic Human Needs.*
[9] ILO, *Meeting Basic Needs;* Jan Tinbergen, *Reshaping the International Order* (London: Hutchinson, 1977); and Sarvodaya Development Education Institute, *Ten Basic Human Needs and Their Satisfaction* (Moxatuwa, 1978).

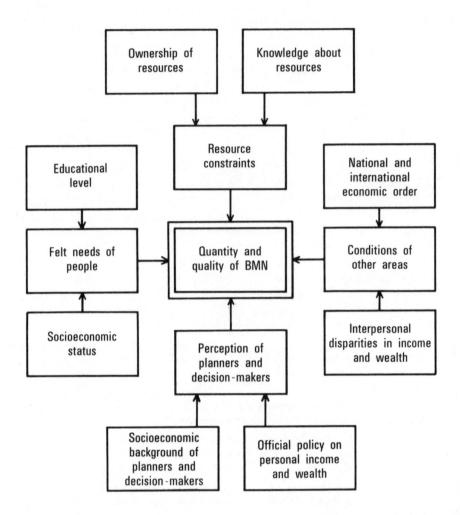

Figure 3-1. Suggested Determinants of Basic Minimum Needs

The term "basic minimum needs" (BMN) implies not merely that there are certain vital needs which in any case must be fulfilled, but also that there is a minimum level of acceptability for such needs. It is, thus, a normative concept. While in a qualitative sense, the categories of needs for any particular society may be defined objectively or subjectively, assigning numerical values to "basic" and "minimum" is, however, a difficult task. Thus, the concept of basic minimum needs implies that there are certain prerequisites for "dignified" living which everyone must possess. The quality_and quantity of such prerequisites are determined by:

1. the level of people's awareness of their own environment;
2. the availability of resources and means for satisfying the needs;
3. the level of development achieved elsewhere and known to the people; and
4. the perception of the planners and decision-makers.

These are illustrated diagramatically in Figure 3–1.

It is, thus, obvious that there is no single list of basic minimum needs applicable to all situations and contexts. Each situation demands an inquiry and analysis before minimum needs can be identified.

The basic minimum needs can be grouped into four types:[10]

1. *Normative needs*: This refers to objective minimum of needs, e.g., minimum level of health care or minimum level of nutrition;
2. *Felt needs of individuals*: This refers to the subjective minimum of needs as perceived by the beneficiaries;
3. *Expressed needs or demands*: This is usually a long list of demands which is poorly correlated with normative or felt needs; and
4. *Comparative needs*: These refer to the imputed needs of a group not in receipt of services, but similar in relevant characteristics to another group already receiving services.

The basic human needs apparently range from basic physiological needs to more complex cognitive needs for self-realization. Thus, "within the category of basic needs, several subcategories are distinguished. It is, for example, proposed to differentiate between "minimum" or "biophysical" and "essential" needs. The former must be satisfied in order to sustain life. The latter are those needs where satisfaction is perceived as indispensable and which when met "are replaced by new needs, also perceived as indispensable."[11]

Basic needs change through time; as lower order needs are satisfied, higher order ones come to the fore. The norms for identifying needs, therefore, cannot be static.

---

[10] I. Bradshaw, "The Concept of Social Need" in *New Society* (30 March 1972); and ILO, *Employment, Growth and Basic Needs*, p. 32.
[11] John R. Mathiason, "Measurement of Basic Minimum Needs" [UN Correspondence Seminar on Local and Intermediate Level Development, Session II, New York, June 1977]. The basic needs according to Mathiason include two elements. First, they include certain minimum requirements of a family for private consumption, adequate food, shelter, and clothing are obviously included, as would be certain household equipment and furniture. Second, they include essential services provided by the government for the community at large, such as safe drinking water, sanitation, public transport, health, and educational facilities.

Needs derived objectively or normatively are referred to as objective needs. These needs are defined in terms of certain standards which are really specifications of what is needed by a given populace at a given point in time. Thus, a minimum daily intake of 2,380 calories per head can be set as a standard for nutrition.[12] Similarly, housing standards may be set in terms of square metres of floor space per person. In India, the minimum floor area of a tenement/house for "slum housing" has been recommended as 180 sq. ft.[13] In order to be realistic, standards must be "empirically derived" for each particular "development setting;" they should not be copied or "airlifted" from elsewhere.

Subjective needs are those which are expressed and articulated by the needy themselves and reflect the state of physical and mental make up. As such, subjectively derived needs not only change but also could be unrealistic. In the developing societies people do not have a clear perception of their needs. In a situation where the aspirations of the people are curbed and where they are indoctrinated about their lowly "place" in the society, the BMNs expressed by them may in fact be far lower than the ones derived normatively. A person who gets only one square meal a day aspires to get two square meals. He fails to see beyond his food requirements. Such cases are not hard to find, especially in the poverty-stricken countries of the world.

Methodologically, the only realistic way of defining BMN is that which fuses the objective and subjective criteria into one. Basic needs could thus, be conceptualized as a construct of objective needs weighted by people's preferences.[14] The basic needs should, therefore, be defined as that set of needs which, given the existing level of socioeconomic development, could be satisfied in the foreseeable future.

Taking all these factors into account we can arrive at the following classification of BMN:

1. Needs which pertain to the three basic necessities of life and have to be provided to each individual/family — food, clothing, and shelter. They also cover drinking water, fuel, etc.
2. Needs which enhance the general welfare of the people and improve the individual's capacity to produce more for his own welfare and which have to be provided only to groups and not to individuals, such as medical care, education, transportation and communication, power, marketing, political, and social institutions, etc.

---

[12] Standard set by the Food and Agriculture Organization of the United Nations.
[13] Ministry of Works and Housing, *Report of the Committee for Slum Clearance Improvement Scheme and the Scheme for Environmental Improvement in Slum Areas* (New Delhi, 1975).
[14] Mathiason, "Measurement of Basic Minimum Needs."

   (b) Value of human capital stock created by schooling (experimental)
       Ratio of mean educational capital in the most educated quintile
       to mean educational capital in the least educated quintile

3. *Income and Consumption*
   (a) Net Beneficial Product per capita (experimental)
   (b) Proportion and number of families below the food poverty threshold (experimental)
   (c) Ratio of mean income of richest quintile to mean income of poorest quintile
   (d) Rate of inflation of consumer prices

4. *Employment*
   (a) Unemployment rate of the totally unemployed, by occupation and by educational attainment
       Underemployment rate in totally unemployed equivalent, by occupation and by educational attainment
   (b) Real wage rate index, skilled versus unskilled workers, by occupation

5. *Nonhuman Productive Resources*
   (a) Reproducible capital stock
   (b) Arable land
       Concentration ratio of agricultural land ownership
   (c) Forested land
   (d) Mineral reserves, by type of mineral

6. *Housing, Utilities, and the Environment*
   (a) Proportion of occupied dwelling units adequately served with water
       Proportion of the population served by electricity at home
   (b) Index of housing adequacy (experimental)
     (i) Proportion of households with 1.5 persons or less per room
     (ii) Proportion of occupied dwelling units made of strong materials
     (iii) Proportion index for Greater Manila (experimental)
   (c) Proportion index for Greater Manila (experimental)
       Pollution concentration levels, by type of pollutant by station
   (d) Proportion of river-lengths polluted by river, by degree of pollution

7. *Public Safety and Justice*
   (a) Crime incidence rate, by type of crime
       Index of citizens' perception of public safety and justice (experimental)
   (b) Backlog of judicial cases
       Ratio of judicial cases disposed to total cases needing disposition, by court of jurisdiction
   (c) Number admitted to penal institutions
       Number confined in penal institutions

8. *Political Values*
   (a) Ratio of votes cast to registered voters
       Ratio of registered to population aged twenty-one and over
   (b) Index of political mobility (experimental)
   (c) Index of political participation (experimental)
       (i) Index of political awareness (experimental)
       (ii) Index of freedom of political dissent (experimental)
   (d) Index of political efficacy (experimental)
9. *Social Mobility*
   (a) Index of gross occupational mobility (experimental)
   (b) Index of perceived social mobility (experimental)

It is clear that each index mentioned above forms a part of the whole such that, taken in isolation, its usefulness may be limited for policy-making. Besides, some acceptable norm may still have to be adopted to derive utility from the indices which will point out whether a particular index may be considered high or low. In any case, the issue of whether the indices should be left alone or to derive a unitary index remains an open question.[20]

In both the United Nations and Development Academy of the Philippines papers referred to earlier, indicators should also be guarded against limitations imposed by quantitative measurement. Based on the same argument generally attached to the difficulty of directly measuring the levels of living, most of the suggested indicators can only be measured quantitatively by indirect method. Hence, nutrition is proposed to be measured by calorie intake and protein intake per capita per day, and learning or education finds its proxy in the school enrolment ratio and the number of years spent in schools.

The implication of the indirect measure could perhaps be appreciated fully if it is used for objective and target setting processes. For example, in the field of education, the objective may be to increase the literacy rate of the country. In terms of targets, this is usually represented by increasing the number of classrooms and teachers. Despite their correlation, literacy cannot be fully reflected in the number of classrooms or teachers.

Nonetheless, the preoccupation with social indicators, is recognized as a clear step towards improving the methods of approximating the state of social welfare, notwithstanding its limitations. This approach enables planners to be concerned not only with the structure of production, but also with the contribution products may give or have towards satisfying the needs of the society.

---

[20] For a discussion of the disadvantages and advantages of a unitary index, see Jan Drewnowski, *Studies in the Measurement of Levels of Living and Welfare* (UNRISD report no. 70.3) (Geneva: United Nations Research Institute for Social Development, 1970).

BASIC NEEDS IN PLANNING: THE CASE OF THE PHILIPPINES

The Concern for Basic Needs

It is interesting to note that the fundamental source of evidence of a country's concern for basic needs is found in its constitution. Thus, among the provisions of Article II of the Constitution of the Philippines are:

> . . . promote social justice to ensure the dignity, welfare, and security of all the people . . . regulate the acquisition, ownership, use, enjoyment, and disposition of private property, and equitably diffuse property ownership and profit.
>
> . . . establish, maintain, and ensure adequate social services in the field of education, health, housing, employment, welfare, and social security to guarantee the enjoyment of the people of a decent standard of living.

The ways to achieve the above concerns are scattered in different laws and statutes of the country. An integrated document which embodies the policies, strategies, programmes, and projects to attain the aims and aspirations of the people, however, is the country's development plan. The Philippines, especially at the national level, has a long tradition in planning. A relevant starting point on how the country perceived the solution to its basic needs situation is, therefore, the present national development plan.

As with other developing countries, the Philippines had promoted growth-oriented industrialization aimed at import substitution until the 1970s. Realizing the futility of the approach, government policy-makers and planners decided to change the strategy in the early 1970s.[21] Economic growth of the Philippines during the period 1946 to 1976 is placed at about 6 per cent per annum in real terms. For the thirty-year period, average per capita income increased by 1.5 times.[22] This relatively satisfactory achievement, however, is dimmed when income distribution figures during the same period are considered. At least, income distribution during the period had remained the same.[23]

---

[21] It was reported that the Philippines came to a dead end in import-substitution production in the latter half of the 1950s, Nagatoshi Suzuki, "Asian Economic Development and Export-Oriented Industrialization" (Special paper, no. 4) (Tokyo: Institute of Developing Economies, 1976) p.5.

[22] Russell J. Cheetham and Edward K. Hawkins, *The Philippines Priorities and Prospects for Development* (Washington, D.C.: World Bank, 1976), p. 11.

[23] Mahar Mangahas and Bruno Barros, "The Distribution of Income and Wealth: A Survey of Philippine Research" (Manila: Philippine Institute for Development Studies, 1979), p. 26; also, Cheetham and Hawkins, *The Philippines*, p. 51.

Table 3-1. Selected Indicators of Social Welfare by Area

	Philippines	Luzon	Visayas	Mindanao
Health and Nutrition				
Number of Hospital Beds per				
10,000 Population (1974)	12	17	8	6
Rural Health Clinics per				
10,000 Population (1974)	.5	.5	.6	.3
Physicians per 10,000 Pop. (1973)	3.2	4.0	2.6	1.6
Life Expectancy In Years (1970)	60.6	60.4	58.9	59.9
Infant Mortality per 10,000				
Live Births (1973)	64.7	62.6	80.4	54.7
Percentage of Families Below Food				
Threshold Level (1975)	44.9	40.9	53.8	43.9
Percentage of Malnourished				
Children to Total Child				
Population (1976)	30.6	30.5	33.6	26.9
Education				
Literacy Rate (1970)	83.5	87.9	79.2	74.3
School Participation Rates (1970)				
Elementary	113	112	113	93
Secondary	50	58	45	35
Housing				
Percentage of Urban Households				
that Cannot Afford Shell				
Housing (1971)	69.1	61.4	89.4	78.1
Percentage of Households Without				
Safe Water (1971)	75.6	56.8	78.7	84.8
Percentage of Households Without				
Toilets (1971)	78.1	69.5	84.2	87.1

SOURCE: National Economic and Development Authority, *Regional Development: Issues and Strategies*, (Regional Planning Studies No. 1) (Manila, 1978), p. 11.

A more disturbing aspect, meanwhile, is the presence or absence of basic social amenities in the different regions of the country. Clearly, as can be discerned from Table 3-1, the Philippines has not much to show with its 6 per cent real economic growth over thirty years. Thus, in 1975, it was estimated that about 45 per cent of the total families in the country were below the food threshold level, and in 1976 the percentage of malnourished children to the total population was estimated at 31 per cent. Housing needs in 1971 were not satisfied either. In urban areas alone, 69 per cent of households could not afford shell housing in 1971.

The same inadequacy was observed in the provision of utilities. Thus, about 76 per cent of the total households in the country in 1971 did not have safe water. Electricity, on the other hand, was available only to about 26 per cent of the country's total households in 1975.

Planning in the Philippines could not be accused of being insensitive to the above mentioned problems. The current five-year Development Plan in particular is addressed:

> . . . toward a direct and purposeful attack against poverty by:
> focussing on the poorest of our society, planning to meet their basic
> nutritional needs, reducing if not eliminating illiteracy, expand-
> ing employment opportunities, improving access to basic social
> services, equalizing opportunities, sharing the fruits of develop-
> ment equitably, and introducing the requisite institutional
> changes.[24]

This shift towards social development permeates at all levels of planning in the country. An operationalization of this concern, on the other hand, came in the form of eleven basic needs espoused by the country's Ministry of Human Settlements. These eleven basic needs are: food, shelter, clothing and cottage industries, water, power, livelihood, education and technology, medical services, sports and recreation, mobility, and the ecological balance. The goal of every region, town, and village of the country is to be at least self-sufficient in these basic needs.

Objectives, Policies, and Strategies of the 1978–82 Plan

The gravity of the socioeconomic problems confronting the country warrants an explicit definition of the aims of society. In this, the government's response includes:

1. Promotion of social development and social justice through the creation of productive employment opportunities, reduction of income disparities, improvements of the living standards of the poor, and enrichment of social and cultural values;
2. Attainment of self-sufficiency in food and greater self-reliance in energy;
3. Attainment of a high and sustained economic growth;
4. Maintenance of an acceptable price level and improvement in domestic resource mobilization and balance of payments position; and
5. Increased development of lagging regions especially rural areas.[25]

[24] Ferdinand E. Marcos, "The Philippine Development Plan: An Instrument for the Democratization of Development" in Cabinet Committee on the Development Plan, *Five-Year Philippine Development Plan, 1978–1982, including the Ten-Year Development Plan, 1978–1987* (Manila, 1977), p. xxx.
[25] Cabinet Committee on the Development Plan, *Five-Year Philippine Development Plan, 1978–1982*, p. 8.

The development strategies designed to achieve the above objectives are two-pronged; first, via the

> attainment of a dynamic and balanced economy, particularly through increased agricultural and industrial production, trade diversification and rationalization, transformation of the energy structure, application of science and technology and proper management of natural resources and environment;

and second,

> more equitable access to social development opportunities and fuller utilization of human resources in nation-building.[26]

While the development strategy placed stress on mobilizing the production capabilities of the economy, a number of policies were designed to spread the benefits of production to the rest of the population. Three policies directly related to the basic needs problem are:[27]

— A policy on regional development which seeks to promote regional balance in economic opportunities.
— A policy on human settlements which deals with the provision of basic amenities and sources of livelihood to urban and countryside areas.
— A policy on integrated social development which covers areas of land reform, health, nutrition, housing, education and culture, manpower development, youth and sports development, children, women and workers welfare, cultural minorities, social security, and other social concerns.

Programmes in the Philippine National Development Plan dealing with the above policy thrust are discussed separately.

Regional Development

The Philippines is characterized by unbalanced regional development. Using Metropolitan Manila as a point of reference, it was found that in 1973 not one of the twelve regions of the Philippines approached 50 per cent of Metropolitan Manila's per capita gross regional domestic product (GRDP). On the other hand, three regions namely, Bicol, Eastern Visayas, and Cen-

---

[26] Ibid.
[27] Ibid. pp. 12—4.

tral Mindanao had a per capita GRDP of only 20 per cent or nearly 20 per cent of the per capita GRDP of Metropolitan Manila. Also, trends of regional per capita GRDP relative to Metropolitan Manila during the 1973 to 1977 period revealed slight deterioration in regional income shares.[28] Without doubt, Metropolitan Manila is the most developed region in the country.

The Philippines 1978–82 Plan, therefore, recognized that a major challenge for regional development is to minimize poverty and redress the uneven distribution of income and basic services both intra- and inter-regionally and among social groups. The plan also recognized the uneven distribution of social infrastructure and services among regions. For example, Metropolitan Manila has the highest concentration of medical personnel and medical facilities, while the regions of Eastern Visayas, Central and Western Mindanao, and Cagayan Valley suffer from lack of such amenities.[29]

To hasten attainment of the country's regional development objectives, a regional development body was established in each region. These regional development bodies coordinate the planning and implementation of regional programmes and projects. Recently, to obtain more focus in regional planning, the regional development bodies formulated a regional development investment programme (RDIP) for each region. These investment programmes translated the regional plans into specific sectoral projects for each designated integrated development area of the region. It is contended by Philippine planners that the area and project specificity of the strategy would make the scheme more responsive to the needs of the population in each part of the region.[30]

Health and Nutrition

Two signs which may be considered critical from the point of view of health and nutrition in the Philippines are:

> . . . Potable water supply benefits only 42 per cent of the total population. Public sewerage system serve only 5 per cent of the total population. Sanitary toilet facilities are installed only in 32 per cent of the total households.[31]

[28] Ibid., p.53, table 3.2.
[29] Ibid., p. 57.
[30] This also means that problem identification should be area specific. For an example in this direction, see Philippine Team, *Philippine Report, Part 3: Barangay Profile* (Working paper, 79—22) (Nagoya: United Nations Centre for Regional Development, 1979).
[31] Ibid., p. 118.

> . . . The nationwide survey conducted in March 1977 revealed
> that of the 4.4 million preschool children weighed, 30.6 per cent
> were suffering from moderate and severe degrees of malnutrition.
> Severe deficiencies in iron, vitamin A, and iodine were also
> found. Recent indications show that the incidence of malnutrition
> has not decreased and that among the disadvantaged groups, the
> nutrition status may have even deteriorated.[32]

The response of the Government to these problems is aggressive. Targets
contained in the Five-Year Plan for both water supply and nutrition are
reproduced in Table 3-2 to show the magnitude of the programmes. During
the 1978–82 period, the Government aims to construct and maintain a host
of waterworks to raise the percentage of total population served from 42 per
cent in 1977 to 62 per cent in 1982, and finally to 83 per cent in 1987. For the
same period, water supply is projected to reach 55 per cent of the rural
population in 1982 from 33 per cent in 1977, and to 80 per cent in 1987. The
water supply of other urban areas, i.e., excluding Metropolitan Manila will
have served 65 per cent of the urban population in 1982, and 85 per cent by
1987. To achieve these targets, the total investment requirements for the
1978–82 period will be about eight billion pesos (1978 prices), and for the
period 1983–87 about ten billion pesos (1978 prices).[33]

Nutrition targets in the Philippine Development Plan revealed the same
highly positive figures. Thus, a reduction from the 1976 level of 0–6 year-
olds suffering from second degree malnutrition was placed at 24.8 per cent to
15.7 per cent in 1982, and finally to 11 per cent in 1987, as projected by the
Government. Those suffering from third degree malnutrition, on the other
hand, will drop from 5.8 per cent in 1976 to 1.8 per cent in 1982 to 0.9 in
1987.

Likewise, malnutrition cases in 7–14 year-olds is projected to decrease
dramatically. For second degree cases, the percentage is targeted to decrease
from 13.3 per cent in 1976 to 3.1 per cent in 1982, and then to 1.2 per cent in
1987. Similarly, the third degree malnutrition cases are expected to drop
from 0.7 per cent in 1976 to 0.2 per cent in 1982 and 0.1 per cent in 1987. To
achieve the targets of the plan, the Government estimated an annual expenditure on health, nutrition, and family planning of 2.44 billion pesos.[34]

[32] Ibid.
[33] Ibid., p. 311, table 15.5.
[34] Ibid., p. 370.

Table 3-2. Targets of Water Supply and Nutrition Programmes of the Philippines, 1978–82 and 1987

	Base 1977	1978	1979	1980	Projected 1981	1982	1987
Water Supply Targets							
1. Metropolitan Manila							
% population served	80	81	81	82	82	83	88
2. Other Urban Areas							
% population served	49	52	55	58	62	65	85
3. Rural Areas							
% population served	33	37	42	46	51	55	80
4. Philippines							
% population served	42	46	50	54	58	62	83
Nutrition Targets	Base Year 1976						
1. 0–6 year olds							
% Second-degree	24.8	21.4	19.8	18.4	17.1	15.8	11.0
% Third-degree	5.8	4.6	3.7	3.0	2.3	1.8	0.9
2. 7–14 year olds							
% Second-degree	13.3	8.2	6.5	5.1	4.0	3.1	1.2
% Third-degree	0.7	0.4	0.3	0.3	0.2	0.2	0.1

SOURCE: Cabinet Committee on the Development Plan, *Five-Year Philippine Development Plan, 1978–1982, including the Ten-Year Development Plan, 1978–1987* (Manila, 1977), pp. 184, 318.

Education

One of the basic objectives of the Government is:

> to provide for a broad general education that will assist each individual to attain his potential as a human being, enhance the range and quality of individual and group participation in the basic functions of society, and acquire the essential educational foundation for his development into a productive and versatile citizen committed to national goals and ideals.[35]

To achieve the above objectives, commitment to the following prerequisites are considered necessary:

> Physical infrastructure and learning resource materials must be distributed well and made easily available. More flexible admission and financial assistance schemes will be developed to fa-

[35] Ibid., p. 203.

cilitate the entry and re-entry of qualified and deserving youths.
In response to the divergent needs of the regions, alternative
educational programmes and delivery systems will have to be
evolved.
In the formal system, staff training and retraining, accreditation
schemes, testing, guidance and counselling will undergo further
improvements. Better systems of school supervision, regulation,
evaluation and promotion of students will be instituted. The nonformal system will be further strengthened by certification requirements of skills standards and guidance counselling for the
out-of-school youth.

The underlined thrust on quality improvement in basic education is
combined with the programme to reach the maximum number of school-age
population. Thus, target participation rates for the school year 1982–83 for
the elementary level is placed at 98 per cent, for secondary level at 60 per cent
and for the tertiary level at 19.3 per cent. For the succeeding school years,
participation rates at the elementary level will remain at 98 per cent,
however, participation rates at the secondary level will increase to 63 per cent
and at the tertiary level to 21.2 per cent during the school year 1987–88.[37]

A complementary programme for the informal education sector also
outlined the following thrusts: (a) providing opportunities for the acquisition
of skills necessary to enhance employability, efficiency, productivity, and
competitiveness in the labour market and (b) providing and ensuring func-
tional literacy, numeracy and general education which will foster the ability
to gain knowledge required for self-realization.

The targets of the nonformal education programmes are: (a) the inexperienced and young clientele (15–24 years old) who will need entry-level
and basic skills, (b) the employed or unemployed elementary or high school
dropouts who would like to re-enter formal education, (c) those fifteen years
old and above, needing compensatory education, and (d) technical and pro-
fessional workers needing skills upgrading.[38]

To implement the programmes calculated to achieve the above goals,
the Government estimated that it needs to invest 25.7 billion pesos during
the 1978-82 period. On an annual basis, investment on education and manpower will rise from 3:5 billion pesos in 1978 to a staggering 7.5 billion pesos
in 1982.[39]

[36] Ibid., pp. 203—4.
[37] Ibid., p. 207.
[38] Ibid., p. 210.
[39] Ibid., p. 370.

Housing

In terms of the hierarchy of man's basic needs in life, the Philippine Plan considered housing as next to food and clothing.[40] The term housing as used, however, does not only mean shelter, but also the improvement of environmental conditions in marginal areas. Alternatively, housing is considered to also involve the development of viable communities with necessary facilities, services, and amenities so that food, nutrition, employment, education, recreation, and culture are integrated into the lives of the residents.[41]

The low and middle income households of the country are the primary targets of the housing programmes in the Philippines. In view of the acute need for housing in urban areas, however, urban households will be given priority. Housing assistance, nevertheless, will be extended to settler families served by the agrarian reform and resettlement programme. Major programmes contained in the plan to be undertaken by the Government in housing include: (a) direct housing, which includes the construction of new units and the development of sites and services in resettlement areas, (b) upgrading of sites and services in marginal areas and in rural areas, and (c) land assembly.

During the 1978–87 period, it is estimated that about 1.1 million households will benefit from direct housing and the upgrading of sites and services. The number of households served during the 1978–82 period is placed at 547,500. The total estimated investment for the 1978–87 period is placed at 42.1 billion pesos, of which 12.9 billion pesos will be for the first five years.[42]

Observations

The Philippine Development Plan for 1978–82 and 1978–87 certainly contained more than what was summarized in the preceding pages. Nevertheless from what was discussed, the following observation may be advanced:

First, the plan is certainly loaded with formal statements regarding the Government's concerns on providing the basic needs of the people. Evidence in this regard is clearly illustrated by the objectives, strategies, and policies in the development plan.

---

[40] Ibid., p. 215.
[41] Ibid.
[42] Ibid., p. 218.

Second, the target figures of the plan indicate in a way the anxiety of the Government to provide basic needs for the maximum number of people as soon as possible. For example, the water supply target is expected to cover 83 per cent of the population from a low of 42 per cent in 1977.

Third, the basic needs programme of the Government, in effect, could be taken as a scheme of income distribution or as an equity-oriented policy. Thus, the nutrition, health and education programmes have all the elements for alleviating the standard of living of the poor.

Fourth, basic needs content of the current plan is actually rooted in the country's planning tradition and is a derivative of the basic concerns of the state. Thus, the question really may not be on whether a state is concerned with basic needs, rather it should be on whether it has the resources and capability to achieve its objectives.

BASIC MINIMUM NEEDS IN NATIONAL PLANNING:[43]
CASE STUDY OF INDIA

Planning in India has always been positive with respect to distributive justice, and has made persistent and conscientious attempts to improve the living conditions of the poor in urban as well as rural areas. The problems of poverty and pestilence inherited by the country in 1947 (year of independence) were, however, so large, that despite the vigorous attempts of the past three decades, no less than 40 per cent of the Indian population still live below the poverty line.

Realizing the enormity of the problem faced by the poor and less privileged people, the Government prepared a package of basic needs programme in the early 1970s and included it in its Fifth Five-Year Plan launched in 1974–75. The objectives set out in this plan were:
1. The provision of facilities for elementary education for children up to the age of fourteen at the nearest possible place from their homes;
2. Ensuring, in all areas, a minimum uniform availability of public health facilities which would include preventive medicine, family planning, nutrition, and the detection of early morbidity and adequate arrangements for treatment;
3. Supplying drinking water to villages suffering from chronic scarcity of having unsafe water sources;

---

[43] For detailed study on basic needs in India, see Indian Team, *Indian Report, Part 2 Needs and Aspirations of Rural Communities; the Social and Economic Milieu and Need Patterns* (Working paper 79–17) (Nagoya: United Nations Centre for Regional Development, 1979).

4. Provision of all-weather roads to all villages having a population of 1,500 persons or more; this minimum limit being conceived of for a cluster of villages in the case of hilly, tribal, and coastal areas;
5. Provision of developed house sites for landless labour in rural areas;
6. Carrying out environmental improvement of slums; and
7. Ensuring the spread of electricity to cover approximately 30–40 per cent of the rural population.

The above is indicative of the accent on social services in India's Basic Minimum Needs Programme. Among the three most basic necessities of life — food, clothing, and shelter — only the last one figured in the programme, and that too, only so far as it related to house sites. It is assumed that food, clothing, and shelter are the responsibilities of individuals; the state can help them get employment and thus, income which could be used to meet these needs. Those facilities and services which can be used by a group of people and for which a community threshold is needed have constituted the core of the basic needs programme in India since 1976–77.

Even though the term National Minimum Need was spelled out clearly only during Fifth Five-Year Plan its various components were being provided even during earlier years. Elementary education, rural health, nutrition, rural water supply, rural roads, house sites for the landless, slum improvement, and rural electrification, were important components of rural and urban development schemes during the 1950s and 1960s.

Table 3-3. Outlay and Expenditure on Minimum Needs Programme 1974–80

(Rs crores)

Sl. No.	Item	1974–79 Outlay	1974–78 Expenditure	1978–79 Outlay	1978–79 Expd.	1979–80 Outlay	1979–80 Expd.
1	Elementary Education	463	230	139	132	88	61
2	Adult Education		1	7	4	13	7
3	Rural Health	296	74	40	33	39	33
4	Rural Water Supply	563	262	114	133	152	188
5	Rural Roads	502	231	120	152	121	182
6	Rural Electrification	282	103	52	34	53	45
7	House sites/Houses for Rural Landless Labourers	109	50	16	22	32	53
8	Environmental Improvement of Slums	105	38	11	10	16	16
9	Nutrition	287	49	26	20	21	22
10	Total	2607	1038	525	540	535	607

SOURCE: Planning Commission, *Sixth Five-Year Plan* (New Delhi, 1981).

The increase in expenditure on various components of the Minimum Needs Programme from Rs10,599.20 million during the fourth plan period (1968–69 to 1973–74) to Rs21,850 million during the fifth plan (1974–75 to 1979–80), was indicative of the seriousness with which the Government undertook the programme. It should, however, be appreciated that India is a vast country with very limited resources for development. The investment of about $3 billion for a population of 600 million in a period of five years is by any standards a meagre amount. It works out to just US$1 per head per annum, although one must add that when it is added up to provide common services, it is not a small amount. Further, the Minimum Needs Programme has its own target group and does not benefit all equally. It is focused on the poor.

It was largely because of the limitations of resources that the Government could not include the three basic necessities of life — food, clothing, and shelter — into the minimum needs package with a firm commitment to implement the same as a time-bound programme. There are other reasons too, the important one being the need to set the national economy moving at a level which alone could make the country, self-reliant in the foreseeable future. The emphasis came to be laid on those needs which were to be shared by a larger number of people — primary education, drinking water, roads, health services, etc.

During the Fifth Five-Year Plan period (1974/75–1979/80), the National Minimum Needs Programme was supplemented by a number of other programmes such as land reforms, community development, intensive rural employment projects, drought prone areas programme, tribal area development programme, small farmers development programme, family welfare and nutrition programme, housing, water supply and sanitation programmes, and special programmes for the development of the hill areas.

The Minimum Needs Programme in India is a national programme. This being the case, only those needs which have relevance all over the country or in major parts of the country have been incorporated in it. It was left to the State Governments to evolve additional programmes based on their own resources. The amounts invested by the various state governments are quite substantial.

By mid-1975 the above provision of the Fifth Five-Year Plan were capsuled into a twenty-point programme, part of which was implemented with great urgency. The points which were relevant to the Basic Minimum Needs package are:

1. Agricultural land ceiling — redistribution of land;
2. Housing sites for the houseless people in rural areas;
3. Abolition of the bonded labour system;

4. Liquidation of rural indebtedness and provision of institutional credit to the poor;
5. Assured minimum wages for agricultural labour;
6. Provision of inexpensive cloth to the common man and development of the handloom sector to provide greater employment opportunities;
7. Socialization of urban land to secure excess land for provision of house sites for the poor;
8. Provision of essential commodities at reasonable prices to the common man.

In fact, the twenty-point programme, notwithstanding its other weaknesses, was perhaps the first major and serious step taken by the Government to improve the living conditions of the poor in India. It did have a desired impact on Indian society.

The new Government formed after the 1977 election by and large, abandoned the twenty-point programme, although it did not abandon the concept underlying it. It laid greater emphasis on employment, especially in the rural areas with the hope that if the people's income increased, their minimum needs would be automatically met. It gave overwhelming importance to adult education. The Government also laid considerable emphasis on decentralization of planning and decision-making. Heroic attempts were made to prepare plans for the lowest level administrative units with a view to involve the people in the development processes. The National Minimum Needs Programme incorporated in the Fifth Five-Year Plan was not abandoned; it was pursued with the same seriousness but with different priorities. The new areas of interest were nutrition, employment and literacy. The Government also announced its determination to do everything possible to create conditions which would improve the quality of life of the people.

The new Government was, however, too inexperienced and unstable to carry out its promises and intentions beyond rhetoric. It set goals which were unrealistic: For example, it wanted to achieve the following within a period of ten years (1977/78–1987/88):

1. the removal of unemployment and significant underemployment;
2. an appreciable rise in the standard of living of the poorest sections of the population;
3. provision by the State of some of the basic needs; especially of the low income groups, like clean drinking water, adult literacy, elementary education, health care, rural roads, rural housing for the landless, and minimum services for the urban slums.

These primary objectives would be attained while:

4. achieving a higher rate of growth of the economy than in the past;

5. moving towards a significant reduction in the present disparities of income and wealth; and

6. ensuring the country's continued progress towards self-reliance.

The plan indicated four areas of emphasis in achieving these objectives — agriculture, cottage and small-scale industries, area planning for integrated rural development, and the provision of minimum needs.[44]

To achieve the above targets, the Government allocated Rs41,800 million for the Basic Needs Programme during the Sixth Five-Year Plan (1978–83) (it terminated the Fifth Five-Year Plan in 1977 and switched over to the system of rolling plan for five years starting with 1978). The components of the BMN programme were:

1. Elementary and Adult Education
2. Rural Health
3. Drinking Water
4. Rural Roads
5. Rural Electrification
6. Housing and Urban Development
7. Nutrition

The Minimum Needs Programme included in the Sixth Five-Year Plan underwent further strengthening and change, when the Congress Party was back in the saddle in 1980. The new Government went back to the five-year period planning process, and reworked the Sixth Five-Year Plan in 1979–80 (the year when the Fifth Five-Year Plan was scheduled to end).

The new Sixth Five-Year Plan has made a provision of Rs58,070 million for the BMN programme, more than doubling the allocation made for it (Rs26,070 million) during the Fifth Five-Year Plan period.

> It is expected that this programme coupled with various other programmes of rural development would enhance opportunities for employment and improve life of the rural poor. A high level machinery for monitoring the implementation of the programme at Central and State levels would need to be set up, which would also ensure improvement in data base. The physical constraints of the programme would be kept under constant review to achieve the stated objectives and effort will be made to overcome them.[45]

The objectives, norms, targets, and outlays for the different components of the programme are given in Table 3-4.

---

[44] Planning Commission (Delhi: Controller of Pub., 1978).
[45] Planning Commission, *Sixth Five Year Plan 1978–83* (New Delhi: Planning Commission, 1981), p. 221.

Allocation of funds for the provision of basic needs during the Sixth Five-Year Plan, when seen spatially, is not uniform. It varies from Rs59 per head (on the basis of 1971 population) for Tamilnadu to Rs1,254 for Andaman and Nicobar Islands. The smaller states have, in general, a larger per capita allocation. Bigger and backward states like Uttar Pradesh and Bihar have Rs96 and Rs74 per capita allocation respectively. For more details of statewide allocations for each component of the BMN, see Table 3-5.

Observations

One can derive some important conclusions from the study of the BMN programme of India.

1. Indian planners and policy-makers have deliberately avoided the controversial BMN approach to planning. Instead, they have concentrated on strengthening the BMN programme articulated in 1953–54.

2. The BMN programme in India is a continuation of the various programmes aimed at helping the poor to secure a better share in the fruits of development. All such programmes were bunched together in 1953, under a comprehensive BMN programme.

3. The BMN programme in India is largely aimed at first meeting those needs of the people which can be called group or community needs. Needs of individuals suffering from acute disabilities like extreme poverty are covered under BMN, as also under several other sector programmes, such as those for small farmers, landless labours, tribal populations, bonded labours, etc.

4. The emphasis of the BMN programme in India is not on doling out funds to the poor or even distributing food, clothing, etc. The emphasis is rather on:
   (a) meeting the communal needs; and
   (b) enabling weaker sections of the population to have better access to employment, productive resources, etc.

5. The allocations for BMN programmes increased, as the national economy further expanded. Thus, national development and human development are interrelated processes; there is no conflict between the two.

Table 3-4. Minimum Needs Programme: Targets and Outlays

(Rs crores)

Head	Objective	Target by 1985	Outlay States/UTs Plan	Outlay Central Plan
Elementary Education	100% enrolment in the age group 6–14 by 1990. It would be supplemented with non-formal education.	95% enrolment in the age group 6–11 and 50% in the age group 11–14. It would be supplemented with non-formal education.	851	54
	100% coverage of adults in the age group 15–35 by 1990 through non-formal education.	Target not fixed.	68	60
Rural Health	1. One Community Health Volunteer for a population of 1,000 or a village by 1990.	To increase the number of Community Health Volunteers from 1.4 lakh as on 1 April, 1980 to 3.6 lakhs.	408	169
	2. Establishment of one subcentre for a population of 5,000 in plains and 3,000 in tribal and hilly areas by 2000 A.D.	To increase the number of subcentres from 50,000 to 90,000 or 75% achievement of the objective.		
	3. One PHC for 30,000 population in plains and 20,000 in tribal and hilly areas by 2000 A.D.	To establish 600 additional PHCs and 1000 SHCs over and above 5,400 PHCs and 1,000 SHCs existing now for achieving about 45% of the number required.		
	4. Establishment of one Community Health Centre for a population of one lakh or one C.D. Block by 2000 A.D.	To establish 174 Community Health Centres, in addition to converting existing 340 upgraded PHCs into Community Health Centres.		
Rural Water Supply		Coverage of all the remaining problem villages by 1985 except in some difficult areas like hilly and desert regions.	1,407	600

Head	Objective	Target by 1985	States/UTs Plan	Central Plan
Rural Roads	Linking up of all remaining villages with a population of 1,500 and above and 50% of the total number of villages with population of 1,000–1,500 by 1990.	To cover about 50% of the total number of villages required to be covered to achieve the objective, i.e., about additional 20,000 villages.	1,165	
Rural Electrification	At least 60% of the villages in each State and Union Territory to be electrified by 1990.	40% of the villages required to be covered to achieve the objective, i.e., additional 46,464 to be electrified.	301	
Housing Assistance to Rural Landless Labourers.	Provision of housing assistance to all landless labour households by 1990. Assistance to include house-site construction materials, drinking water well for a cluster of houses and approach road.	To cover all the remaining house-holds for allotment of house-sites and 25% of the eligible house-holds, i.e., about 3.6 million for provision of assistance for construction of houses.	354	
Environmental Improvement of Urban Slums.	100% coverage of the urban slum population by 1990. Facilities to include water supply, sewerage, paving of streets, storm water drains, community latrines. Areas particularly scavengers would be given priority.	40% of the remaining slum population, i.e., additional 10 million slum population to be covered.	151	
Nutrition		*SNP:* 5 million children in 600 ICDS blocks and 5 lakh women to be covered by providing integrated services of feeding, health, welfare, etc. *MDM:* The existing level of beneficiaries, i.e., about 17.4 million children to be continued and the programme to be integrated with other essential services.	219	
		Total	4,924	883

SOURCE: Planning Commission, *Sixth Five-Year Plan* (New Delhi, 1981), p. 226.

Table 3-5. Minimum Needs Programme, States and Union Territories 1980–85

(Rs lakhs)

States/UTs	Rural Electrification	Rural Roads	Elementary Education	Rural Health	Rural Water supply	Rural Housing	Environmental Improvement of Slums	Nutrition	Total	Per Capita Allocation (in Rs)
1 Andhra Pradesh	420	1,500	3,850	2,439	9,500	7,675	800	1,100	27,284	63
2 Assam	3,500	3,600	5,250	1,200	3,000	1,000	75	270	17,895	123
3 Bihar	3,304	14,000	11,000	3,627	7,500	1,100	410	1,000	41,941	74
4 Gujarat	364	13,500	3,500	2,009	6,500	3,085	500	1,650	31,108	117
5 Haryana		350	2,100	853	8,000	990	380	400	13,073	130
6 Himachal Pradesh	240	3,500	822	500	3,500	25	40	117	8,744	250
7 Jammu & Kashmir	250	1,600	1,950	903	4,500	100	440	120	9,863	215
8 Karnataka	140	4,500	3,000	2,003	1,900	5,500	1,500	2,243	20,786	71
9 Kerala		1,300	1,650	954	4,500	1,200	600	1,400	11,604	55
10 Madhya Pradesh	4,855	4,000	6,460	3,607	6,000	2,900	800	2,000	30,622	75
11 Maharashtra		9,400	3,300	3,000	23,000	3,500	1,400	2,600	46,200	92
12 Manipur	376	1,000	600	527	1,750		25	110	4,388	400
13 Meghalaya	318	520	520	443	1,950		30	125	3,906	390
14 Nagaland	126	325	480	297	1,175			130	2,533	506
15 Orissa	2,034	3,000	2,800	1,600	3,400	800	100	650	14,384	65
16 Punjab		2,000	2,200	1,377	6,800	1,200	500	80	14,157	104

(Rs lakhs)

States/UTs	Rural Electrification	Rural Roads	Elementary Education	Rural Health	Rural Water supply	Rural Housing	Environmental Improvement of Slums	Nutrition	Total	Per Capita Allocation (in Rs)
17 Rajasthan	2,810	6,500	6,900	1,743	10,629	475	250	327	29,634	115
18 Sikkim	60	900	390	139	600	15	15	125	2,229	
19 Tamil Nadu		7,000	2,400	2,182	5,000	2,500	2,500	2,600	24,182	59
20 Tripura	229	1,100	940	336	1,200	100	50	580	4,535	283
21 Uttar Pradesh	8,879	31,500	11,300	7,489	22,000	1,800	1,000	883	84,851	96
22 West Bengal	1,388	3,750	12,750	2,588	4,800	1,200	2,700	2,500	31,676	72
Total – States	29,293	114,845	84,162	39,816	137,204	35,150	14,115	21,010	475,595	
U.Ts.										
1 Andaman & Nicobar Islands	90	450	434	44	405	5		15	1,443	1,254
2 Arunachal Pradesh	568	300	2,720	400	1,277			50	5,315	1,138
3 Chandigarh		10	418	85				125	638	248
4 Dadra and Nagar Haveli		40	70	37	60	10		20	237	320
5 Delhi		30	2,950	12	700	45	920	450	5,107	126
6 Goa, Daman & Diu		25	380	55	170	50	75	40	795	92
7 Lakshadweep		10	58	22	13			5	108	337
8 Mizoram	154	720	520	326	800			50	2,570	774
9 Pondicherry		60	195	49	82	90	35	109	620	132
Total – UTs	812	1,645	7,745	1,030	3,507	200	1,030	864	16,833	
Grand Total	30,105	116,490	91,907	40,846	140,711*	35,350	15,145	21,874	492,428*	90

NOTE: *In addition Rs600 crores are provided for accelerated Rural Water Supply Programme under the Centrally Sponsored Scheme.
SOURCE: Planning Commission, *Sixth Five-Year Plan* (New Delhi, 1981) p. 227.

BMN APPROACH TO PLANNING: SOME CONCLUSIONS

Considerable amount of literature exists on the so-called BMN approach to development planning. What in essence it means is that development planning in the developing countries should be geared mainly to the provision of basic needs of the people. Some experts have gone even to the extent of identifying technologies relevant to the BMN approach to planning. It is contended that advanced technology, large-scale projects, modern industries, and centralized planning do not help solve the problem of poverty. Rather, they further accentuate it because the social system in the developing countries so operates that all of these benefits go to those who are already well-off. What helps the poor are appropriate technologies, small-scale projects, cottage and small-scale industries, and decentralized planning and development from below.

While it is readily agreed that there is need for change in the style of development and that greater and more attention needs to be given to the basic needs of the people, no country has so far opted for the Basic Needs approach to planning. There is no doubt that the social welfare or BMN component in national development plans has been strengthened progressively. Three factors appear to account for this. First, the poorer sections of the societies of these countries have become more restive now than before and, hence, the national governments are forced to pay greater attention to them. Secondly, the governments themselves have to win over the poor majority to stay in power. And thirdly, it is easier to get assistance from developed countries and international agencies for the so-called basic needs items than for the development of agriculture, industry, infrastructure, etc.

Neither the Philippines nor India has made any major change in its development strategies in response to increased glorification of the basic needs strategy of development. This applies to other countries too. In fact, there is growing hostility against the so-called Basic Needs approach or strategy of development, even though no one is against the idea of including Basic Needs as a major component of development.

Why is it so? Is it because there is something wrong with the developing countries? Are they less concerned about the poor, than the developed countries are? Or is there something wrong with the so-called Basic Needs strategy itself? Does it not give a smell of a new fad which is too simplistic to be useful? Does it really answer the problems of the developing countries — the problem of national survival; the problem of low productivity; the problem of disjointed economic systems; the problem of growing poverty; and many others?

Whether we like it or not, development, for quite some time to come, has to be seen from two different though interrelated angles: (a) development of a nation state, and (b) development of the people. For the last three decades, the first was in the forefront; and the second was treated as its derivative. The approach was undeniably unrealistic. National development should and ought to give due importance and priority to human development. Instead, development as evident from the GDP growth, was given top priority. The welfare of the people was considered as the derivative of the GDP. It was presumed that the growing GDP would automatically improve the peoples' welfare.

The assumption would have been proven right had the sociopolitical factors been favourable, i.e., had the developing societies been structurally more egalitarian and less feudal. The net result was that the GDP grew, in many if not all the developing countries, but the incidence and degree of poverty increased almost universally. The benefits of development were passed on to those who were in a better position to benefit from them.

The call for a new approach to development with BMN as the rallying point was a reaction against the time-honoured Western style development process. It is Western in style because it is based on the experience of Western industrialized countries. Being a reaction, it had to make a frontal attack on its "enemy" and to offer a heavenly bliss to its adherents. It tried to debunk the Western model of development by highlighting its real as well as apparent weaknesses and suggesting a way out of the mess — the BMN approach to development.

The idea that it is the people who ultimately matter and if their welfare is enhanced, the country has developed, is indisputable. It is an ideal which all countries of the world should try to reach. But unfortunately, we are not living in an ideal world. We live in a real world, which is divided into various camps often with dubious and ulterior motives. The basic unit that constitutes the United Nations today is not the human beings; it is the nation state. This basic unit has its strengths and weakness; its autonomy and dependence; its long-term and short-term goals; its perception of the world of today and tomorrow; its organization and governance system; and above all its whims and fancies. These are the important inputs that govern international order. It is not the individuals who shape the world; it is their collective wisdom which shapes it. Unfortunately, it is the nation state through which the collective wisdom is expressed today.

A nation state represents the collective will of its people — but only in the long run. In the short-run, there is disjunction between what the nation state does, and what the people think. The perceptions of the two are different. Each tries to win over the other, but rarely do the views of the two coincide. The difference between a democratically elected government and a dictatorial one is that in the former there are greater points of convergence than in the latter. Moreover, in the former, the nation state has respect for what the people have to say; in the latter, people become tools in the hands of the ruling class.

While thinking of styles and approaches to development, one has to keep the above reality in view. By this we do not mean to say that all that is real is also moral and right. The reality is emphasized only because nothing meaningful and lasting can be achieved without full cognizance of it. We, therefore, propose to examine the Basic Needs approach to development in the light of the circumstances in which the developing countries are trying to develop their economies.

If the experience of the last three decades is any guide, there is no possibility of convergence of views on the approach to development between the North and the South. It is now quite clear that developed countries are not likely to promote a style of development which would diffuse their power base. They see developing countries as huge markets for their industrial products and also as theatres of future small and big wars. If one surveys the disturbing events of the last three decades, especially the localized wars fought between two developing countries, it is clear that the opposing parties responsible for the events were nothing but proxies of the developed countries. The reluctance of the developed countries to transfer advanced technology to developing countries, and the drying sources of aid, are all indicators of what the developed countries aim at.

It is not a mere coincidence that the reluctance of the developed countries to assist the developing countries, the call for a new economic order, and the emphasis on the BMN approach to development, started almost simultaneously. The call for a new economic order was the response of the developing countries to the reluctance of the developed countries to help them modernize their economies and the persistent effort by the DCs to destabilize the LDCs. The BMN approach to development was meant to achieve the following objectives: First, it emerged from a genuine concern of social scientists and others about the way development processes were operating in the developing countries. It was increasingly realized that the meaning of development must change and the best measure of development must be man himself. Second, it was an indirect attack on the goal of self-reliance which many developing countries had initiated and which threatened the existing international economic order. It is pertinent to note that the BMN panacea was meant exclusively for developing countries (even though poverty is found in developed countries too). It had no matching prescription for rich countries which are the main producers of lethal arms and ammunition. And third, the BMN approach, as it finally emerged (irrespective of what the